ALPHA PLAN

Dr David Lewis, D.Phil, BSc (Hon), FIDS, is a psychologist, lecturer, broadcaster and the author of many books on psychology. He is a director of Stresswatch, a non-profit-making company which assists people with stress and anxiety problems; he is a founding trustee of Action on Phobias, a charity involved in establishing self-help groups for men and women with phobic difficulties; and he is technical director of Children Unlimited, an organisation which helps parents take a more active role in their children's education. He has spent the past ten years working on the creation of procedures for the expansion of intellectual and emotional performance and he is especially interested in the application of these methods in education, commerce and industry. He lives in Sussex.

THE
ALPHA PLAN

Making the Most of Your Mind

DAVID LEWIS

A Methuen Paperback

First published in Great Britain in 1986
by Methuen London Ltd
11 New Fetter Lane, London EC4P 4EE

Copyright © 1986 by David Lewis
Illustrations by Richard Armstrong

Made and printed in Great Britain

British Library Cataloguing in Publication Data

Lewis, David 1942–
   The Alpha plan: making the most of your mind.
   1. Self-actualization   2. Self-culture
   I. Title
   158'.1   BF637.S4

ISBN 0–413–59740–7

The Alpha Plan is dedicated to the memory of the late C. Maxwell Cade, whose pioneering studies in biofeedback and mind control have been a source of inspiration and understanding to so many.

Contents

Acknowledgements

My special thanks are due to the many volunteers who have participated in the research on which the Alpha Plan is based, for their patience and enthusiasm. I am especially grateful to my research associate Shandy Mathias for her organisational ability and contribution to the program. I should also like to acknowledge the valuable technical contributions made by Stephen Killick and Andrew Hunt, of K & H Systems, who designed and constructed the specialist bio-monitoring and control equipment employed in the research.

'Whatever the mind of man can conceive and believe it can achieve.'

Clement Stone

PART ONE

Introduction

When early explorers set foot on some alien shore, one of the first things they did was map their new territory. Often their efforts produced no more than rough sketches of the terrain, full of errors and with vast tracts devoid of detail except, perhaps, for a fanciful note about unicorns or dire warnings that 'here be dragons'.

Yet, despite their crudeness, inaccuracies and fantastic embellishments, these early charts were essential to the exploration and understanding of terra incognito. For without them there was no guide, no sense of direction and hence no possibility of making a purposeful voyage of exploration.

Modern explorers of the human mind face a similar predicament. We have our charts of the brain, assembled from a score of different sources: from dissection and microscopic examination; from studies of the results of injuries and natural traumas such as strokes. The brain has been investigated through its anatomy, neurophysiology, psychology, ethology, biophysics and biochemistry. Maps of the brain have been created using techniques such as X-rays, computed tomography and nuclear magnetic resonance. More recently, the brain's electrical activity has been measured with increased accuracy and sophistication, allowing scientists to watch the processes of thought as they occurred – although without, it has to be added, being able to interpret those thoughts.

'A neuroscientist used to be like a man in a Goodyear

blimp floating over a bowls game,' remarks Dr Floyd Bloom of the Scripps Clinic in La Jolla, California. 'He could hear the crowd roar . . . now we're down in the stands. It's not too long before we'll be able to tell why one man gets a hot dog and one man gets a beer.'[1]

And yet, despite this optimistic view, most brain researchers agree that, although they may be a great deal better informed about the structure of the brain, they are not – to paraphrase a remark by the barrister F. E. Smith – much the wiser about the fine print of its functions. Indeed, some hold the pessimistic view that were the brain simple enough for us to comprehend it would be too primitive to permit any such understanding!

Confronted by the paradoxes and puzzles of the brain, each generation of mind researchers has sought refuge in analogy, typically comparing its workings to the most complicated artifacts of their era.

René Descartes, the seventeenth-century French philosopher and mathematician, likened brain function to hydraulically operated statues in the gardens of the Royal Palace at Saint-Germain. He wrote:

> There is a reasoning soul in this machine [the body]; it has its principal site in the brain where it is like the fountaineer who must be at the reservoir, whither all the pipes of these machines are extended, when he wishes to start, stop or in some other way alter their actions.

For early twentieth-century researchers the model was that of a telephone switchboard; while following the Second World War the most compelling comparison was with the servomechanisms and feedback loops of cybernetic guidance and control systems.

[1]G. Maranto, 'The Mind Within the Brain', *Discover* (1984) May issue p. 37.

With the arrival of digital computers the analogy changed yet again. Now the brain was said to resemble an information-processing system in which a single computer co-ordinated inputs and outputs. Later still, as the split-brain theory developed – in which the right and left hemispheres are held to possess different specialised functions – this analogy was modified to portray it as a dual-processing computer.

By the early 1980s, a consensus among brain researchers was that thought processes could most usefully be likened to a network of interconnecting computers, each with its own highly specialised processing function, such as language, short-term memory, vision, hearing, taste, touch, smell and so on.

Certain of these areas have been explored in some detail, with the firings of individual nerve cells being measured during experiments in which one part of the system, for example sight, is stimulated. Others remain virtually uncharted and more mysterious than the planets in our solar system. The frontal portions (lobes) of the brain, for example, seem to specialise in data integration, drawing together information from the various senses, as well as specialising in long-term planning, predicting, anticipating, and creating mental models of the outside world.

For some people, likening brains to computers will seem an unattractively, perhaps even dangerously, dehumanising view and, so long as our ideas of machines and mechanisation are derived from the clockwork automata of the Victorian parlour or the engines of Fritz Lang's *Metropolis*, such concern is scarcely surprising. As Margaret Boden, reader in philosophy and psychology at the University of Sussex, points out, 'the image of "machine" that is currently popular has no place for human values or for the specifically human self-image associated with them.'

But, as Margaret Boden also suggests, there is

another view of machines, an image derived from Artificial Intelligence (AI) studies, which clearly demonstrates 'the potentialities inherent in mechanism to be far greater than could previously have been supposed on the basis of extant machines.'[1]

There are, of course, many important differences between the brain and the computer, some of which are considered in Chapter Three, and it would be dangerous to become too firmly trapped in the analogy.

As Alan Gevins, director of the EEG Systems Laboratory at Langley Porter Neuropsychiatric Institute at the University in San Fransisco, cautions: 'The brain is more complicated than our machines. Until the next technology comes along, it's convenient to model it after local computer networks, but the brain is basically a different sort of entity.'[2]

My own voyage of exploration started some ten years ago through an interest in agoraphobia, a phobic condition named from the Greek word *agora*, meaning the market-place. Sufferers have an intense dread of going, especially unaccompanied, to shopping centres, supermarkets, crowded streets or any other places where people gather. In some cases these fears are so powerful that the victim becomes virtually housebound.

Here were perfectly healthy, intelligent, and previously mobile men and women who – slowly or suddenly – found themselves quite unable to make unaccompanied trips away from home. They knew how to walk down the street, make purchases in supermarkets, pay at check-outs and perform all the other 101 humdrum tasks which make up the normal, domestic routine. And yet they were incapable of doing so. Why?

[1]M. Yazdani and A. Narayanan (eds) (1984) *Artificial Intelligence – Human Effects*; Chichester, Ellis Horwood, p. 197.
[2]K. Stein, 'Brainstorms', *Omni Magazine* (1981) Vol. 4., p. 58.

At about the same time I became involved with developing and running a training programme aimed at enhancing the intellectual development of young children. A particular focus of concern for us were children who had failed in school, who had, for various reasons, found it impossible to master lessons which had been grasped, with varying degrees of ease and expertise, by their companions: they couldn't do sums, read fluently, spell correctly or write legibly.

In contrast to agoraphobics, who were unable to do things they knew how to do (i.e. go shopping, travel on buses etc.), these youngsters were unable to do things because not only did they not know how to do them, but also they refused to believe they would ever be able to learn how to do them. Apart from the obviously circular explanation that their failure to learn was due to stupidity, as evidenced by their failure to learn, why should this be? And why was it that a child who might be quite hopeless at lessons in school had no difficulty in acquiring skills or knowledge in subjects – away from the classroom – which aroused their interest and curiosity?

In 1982 I was invited by Charter Medical to develop and run a series of weekly training workshops at their short-stay mental hospital in London. Their patients are men and women with a wide range of problems, ranging from alcoholism to depression. Many hold highly responsible jobs in industry, commerce and the professions. Often their difficulties appear directly related to the pressures under which they have worked.

The idea behind the workshops was both to provide a stimulating form of occupational therapy and, it was hoped, to equip them with a new set of mind skills – more efficient ways of learning, problem-solving, decision-making and so on – which might help them to work more effectively, and less stressfully, when they returned to their desks.

In seeking answers to the problems faced by phobics and school-children, I derived the concepts of brain function which underly the Alpha Plan. The practical procedures were developed both from my early training workshops and work with a non-clinical population both in Europe and the United States. I have found that Alpha-Plan procedures can considerably enhance major aspects of cognitive performance, reducing stress, eliminating unnecessary anxiety and improving intellectual function over a wide range of tasks for people from all walks of life, not just those with problems. As I explain in Chapter One, groups and individuals participating in the program have included teachers, company executives, scientists and engineers, and members of the armed forces, police and medical professions.

The individual procedures taught in the five-step action plan are not, at least conceptually, new. The discovery that physical relaxation produces a state of emotional calmness (see Step One of the program) was made about half a century ago by the American clinician Edmund Jacobson.

The historical roots of the Zen meditative technique proposed for generating alpha waves (see Step Two of the program) reach back centuries, to Eisai (1145–1215) and Sodo (1200–53), and before them to the ancient Hindu method of attaining enlightenment.

The use of imagery in clinical training can be traced to Pierre Janet's discovery, at the turn of the century, that the *idées fixes* of hysterical patients might be overcome through the substitution of one image for another. Alfred Binet, the founder of intelligence testing, developed what he termed the 'dialogue method' during which patients were encouraged to converse with visual images while introspecting. Much more recently, Richard M. Suinn of Colorado State University has employed what he terms visuomotor behavioural rehearsal (VMBR). The procedure taught in this program, the Alpha Plan, (see Step Four), which I have called mind-mirroring, differs somewhat from VMBR, however, both in the emphasis placed on creating scenes which involve many sensations – taste, touch, sound, smell etc. – in addition to the visual images, and in the way in which mirroring is used to explore, in fantasy, different behavioural and emotional options.

Further, the procedure described in Step Three (performance analysis) of the program owes something to the analytical procedures developed for investigating failures in complex systems.

The originality of the Alpha Plan lies not, therefore, in the development of any specific procedures, but rather in the modification, adaptation and integration of clinically proven techniques and their presentation in a form which makes possible their use through self-help.

This book is divided into three parts. In the first I outline the ideas behind the Alpha Plan and explain some of the reasons why I believe it is possible continuously to enhance human performance. Part Two contains the five-step training program. You can, if you wish, embark upon this immediately without waiting to gain the knowledge provided in the earlier chapters. However, I strongly advise you to read these, at some point, since an understanding of the Alpha Plan's conceptual foundations will make it easier to appreciate the contribution made by each step of training.

In my experience there are four aspects of performance of particular concern to the sort of people interested in this type of self-improvement. These are: learning and studying – ways of remembering and recalling information rapidly and accurately even when working under pressure; decision-making – arriving at the best choice when confronted by complex options; problem-solving, especially in so-called 'divergent' tasks where there is no single, correct, solution; and physical fitness.

This last may seem a curious, perhaps somewhat anomalous, addition to a program whose main purpose is to enhance mental functioning. Yet, as I point out in Part Three, the brain is only able to operate with peak efficiency when the body is fit and well.

For example, it has been found that a common head-cold impairs hand-eye co-ordination more significantly than a moderate amount of alcohol, while influenza greatly reduces powers of concentration. The more resistant the body is to such minor ailments and the greater one's physical stamina and good health (here used in the original sense of 'wholeness'), the more successfully one can confront intellectual challenges and the more efficiently the brain may be employed.

Step Three of the program, in which you learn how to carry out a careful analysis of both the strengths and weaknesses of your current approach to demanding activities, may well pin-point difficulties in learning, decision-making or problem-solving. Equally you may already feel that some, or all, of these are areas where you would like to think more effectively. In either case you should incorporate these practical procedures into your training from Step Three onwards.

I do hope that you will find the ideas which underlie the Alpha Plan interesting and the procedures taught of practical value. I believe that there is an urgent need for us to find ways of using the brain more successfully, as the demands imposed by society grow daily more taxing and the likely penalties for failure increasingly severe.

The story is told of a millionaire who devoted his life and his fortune to seeking the world's greatest philosopher. He died with his quest unfulfilled and, in heaven, asked St Peter to satisfy his curiosity. The saint pointed downwards to an elderly cobbler seated at his bench.

'But he is just a humble shoe-maker,' protested the millionaire. 'I've often sent my boots to him for repair.'

'What you say is perfectly true,' acknowledged St Peter. 'But had that man's life been different he *would* have been the world's greatest philosopher.'

The saddest phrase in any language is, surely, 'what might have been'. For, as Clement Stone so perceptively remarked, we are capable of achieving whatever we can conceive and believe. Failures, therefore, are far more often a consequence of having too limited a vision of one's capacity to succeed and too little faith in one's ability to achieve, than of any in-built intellectual or emotional inadequacies.

My hope, therefore, is that the Alpha Plan will encourage you to expand your vision so that the world becomes a place filled with more possibilities than impossibilities, while at the same time helping to confirm a perfectly justified belief in your brain's boundless potential.

ONE
Your Boundless Brain

*'We're simply so accustomed to the marvels of
everyday thought that we never wonder about it.'*
Marvin Minsky *Why People Think Computers Can't*

The brain has been described as the only general-
purpose computer which can be run on glucose and
made entirely by unskilled labour! Unfortunately, it is
also the only computer that's delivered without any
operating instructions. As a result we have to learn how
to make it work as we go along.

Most people do this with reasonable efficiency and
are said to have average intelligence. A minority who
discover how to make their brain function even more
effectively are described as highly intelligent, while
those who never use it to best advantage are considered
to be stupid. But it's important to realise that these
variations in mental performance are due to the efficiency with which the human biocomputer is used. For
all practical purposes your brain's potential is boundless. The extent to which this tremendous intellectual
potential is realised depends, primarily, on how well
you put your brain to work.

I have called the practical training programme by
which you can make the most of your mind the Alpha
Plan. The purpose of this book is to explain how this
plan can help you achieve peak performance in any
activity.

The Alpha Plan In Action

During the past ten years I have worked with many hundreds of men, women and children – both individually and in groups – helping them become more successful across the whole spectrum of human endeavour, intellectual, emotional and physical.

The areas of mental and physical performance where the Alpha Plan has proved particularly valuable include:

* Learning and studying
* Problem-solving and decision-making
* Playing sports
* Improving physical health
* Enhancing emotional well-being

Let's take each of these in turn to see how such training might help and why it may be necessary.

Learning and Studying

The tremendous growth in knowledge has led to an urgent need for improved learning and studying skills. To pass vital examinations, gain worthwhile employment, achieve promotion, or prepare for a career change it is essential to learn rapidly and recall accurately, even when working under pressure.

If you've been let down by your ability to learn, to study or to recall important information, and if you sometimes doubt whether your mind is capable of coping with new challenges, I've got some good news and some bad news.

The good news is that your brain has the capacity to handle any amount of learning. It has been calculated that our memories could acquire eleven new facts every second of life for more than seventy years and still have ample storage-space in reserve.

The bad news is that the quantity of information the average person needs to make sense of, and enjoy success in, a rapidly changing world is increasing all the time. One can no longer expect to acquire sufficient knowledge and skills when young to last the rest of one's life.

Typical of the problems which people bring to Alpha-Plan workshops was the complaint, by a 42-year-old manager with a multinational computer company, that he found it impossible to keep up with new techniques and procedures: 'My firm is very keen on training and I attend seminars, lectures and conferences several times a year', he explained. 'I feel swamped by facts. The pressure is unrelenting. My brain can't take it all in.'

A science student grumbled that she was doomed to fail her final exams because the demands of the course were more than her memory could cope with. 'I look at the pile of books, think of the mountains of facts I'm supposed to learn and know I'll never remember them all. I've lost all confidence in myself.'

Traditional, school-taught, ways of learning are simply not capable of meeting the demands of modern society. New ways of retaining and recalling large quantities of complex information, rapidly and accurately, must be acquired.

My experience has been that Alpha-Plan procedures bring about a significant enhancement in all aspects of learning as well as helping overcome the effects of stress and anxiety while attempting to study.

Problem-solving and Decision-making

Finding answers and making choices are difficulties which confront us daily. As the world becomes more complicated the demands on us to discover the best possible solutions and take reasoned choices increase. At the same time the probable consequences of mistakes become even more serious and costly.

The production manager of a pharmaceutical company explained that anxiety over errors had caused him sleepless nights and a marked loss of confidence when at work: 'A few years ago I might have taken a chance and hoped for the best,' he explained, 'but now I think of everything that might go wrong and freeze.'

Decision-making against deadlines was a major problem for the creative director of a New York advertising agency. He explained that his concentration and memory seemed to collapse whenever he tried to decide on an important issue: 'It's as if my brain was refusing to pay attention to the facts and figures necessary for arriving at the correct choice,' he explained.

I rank this area of intellectual challenge second on my list of thinking skills that can be enhanced by the Alpha Plan because – after learning – it is the area of mental performance most critical to happiness and success. As the French philosopher Jean-Paul Sartre has said, 'I am my choices . . .'

Playing Sports

The benefits to be gained from the Alpha Plan are not limited to intellectual activities. Its procedures have proved equally helpful for improving performance when playing almost any kind of sport, whether as an amateur or professional.

If you are learning a new sport the Plan will help you to achieve a high level of skill and confidence more quickly and easily. For experienced players the Alpha Plan offers a chance to fine-tune performance.

Its procedures will improve hand-eye co-ordination, reduce errors while performing rapid sequences of complex movements – for instance striking a fast-moving ball – decrease reaction time and enhance concentration. The Alpha Plan also helps one play sport, especially under competitive conditions, in a state of relaxed alertness, freed from the negative influences of needless anxiety.

Improving Physical Health

The Alpha Plan can help improve and protect your health by strengthening the body's natural defence mechanisms. At the same time it safeguards you against such stress-related conditions as high blood pressure, tension-induced headaches, back pains and muscle cramps. Its procedures will allow you to fall asleep more easily and awaken fully rested.

Emotional Health

Although I have left the enhancement of emotional health until last, this is certainly not because I consider it the least important aspect of mental functioning. On the contrary, how we feel exerts a tremendous influence not only on our physical and mental wellbeing, but also on how well we learn, solve problems and make decisions.

Perhaps the most common emotional difficulty people bring to my attention is that they feel needlessly anxious when either performing, or attempting to perform, some activity. A 25-year-old assistant production manager working for a frozen-food company explained:

> My greatest problem is presenting my ideas during managerial discussions. I want to argue against somebody's proposals, or put forward ideas of my own, but although I know exactly what I want to say before the meeting, or what I

ought to have said after it's too late, at the time I usually feel too anxious to make any contribution. My stomach starts churning, my throat goes dry, and I can feel my heart racing. At the same time, I forget the key points of my argument. When I do try and speak I know that what I say is often rambling and off the point, but I'm so nervous it's impossible for me to concentrate.

'Each time my boss makes unreasonable demands on my time I'm determined to assert myself,' the 28-year-old sales manager of an engineering works remarked. 'But when it comes to the crunch, I hold my tongue, take on the extra workload and then feel bitter and guilty for days after.'

Anxiety, fear, frustration, an inability to assert oneself in social or work situations, a lack of motivation or confidence, a failure to cope with life's demands – all are symptoms of a breakdown in emotional well-being.

While the Alpha Plan doesn't claim to provide an antidote to all of life's emotional difficulties, experience has shown that the procedures enhance motivation and self-confidence, while reducing anxiety, so making it much easier to deal positively and effectively with stressful challenges.

The Performance Cycles

The relationship between the five elements of effective mental performance is illustrated on the next page.

As you can see, efficient learning leads to improved problem-solving and decision-making, since you now have more and better information with which to work. This increases confidence, reduces anxiety and makes success more likely than failure. Success, in turn, enhances physical and emotional health, so making it easier for you to acquire new information, and start the

The positive performance cycle

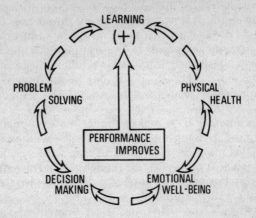

cycle all over again. Unfortunately, one can also get trapped in a negative cycle, with failure in any one area of performance often leading to a more general decline in attainment.

The negative performance cycle

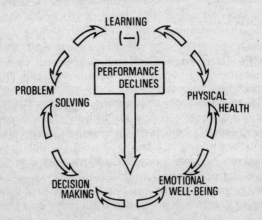

A run of poor decisions, for instance, may make you feel angry, frustrated, or depressed and cause a loss of self-confidence. These negative feelings, when sufficiently strong and sustained, undermine physical and mental performance, so deepening the downward negative cycle.

The Alpha Plan enables you to break out of this failure trap, and develop a positive, achievement-orientated approach to all aspects of living.

The Five-stage Program

The Alpha Plan compares the brain to a computer and views any failure to perform in a desired manner as a software rather than a hardware fault. By software, I mean the set of instructions which enable hardware, that is the brain itself, to function. We will be taking a detailed look at these important terms in Chapter Three. For the moment, however, I just want to provide an overview of the Alpha Plan, and describe the easily mastered five-step training program for enhancing mental and physical performance.

Where to Begin

The starting-point is to identify, clearly and precisely, what is going wrong and why. You will find a full explanation on how this can be done in Step Three of the training.

Care must be taken over this since, typically, we devote very little time to exploring faults in performance. Sometimes this is because we are embarrassed by what we said and did and find it easier, and a lot less distressing, simply to forget what happened. 'I don't even want to think about it,' is a typical response from both adults and children after a particularly humiliating experience.

And if we do attempt to reflect on our failures, it's usual to describe what happened in an entirely negative way, suggesting that everything was done badly and nothing went even half right. 'That was terrible,' sighs the business executive after ruining an important presentation to clients, 'I just couldn't say or do anything right.' 'My game went to pieces,' moans the golfer after getting knocked out of a tournament by a less talented opponent, 'I never played a stroke right.'

However, by dismissing all that was done in this sweeping manner, important clues about how we might do better the next time are ignored. Typically, however disappointing our performance may have been and no matter how far short it fell of our expectations, it will have included good as well as bad features.

The Alpha Plan teaches you how to analyse your performance objectively and accurately so as to identify the true causes of failure, so that such errors may be avoided in future, while identifying and building on any positive features.

With the problem clearly stated, the next two stages involve placing body and mind into a state most receptive to fresh instructions. Because these skills take longer to master than do the procedures for identifying problems, you will be starting work on them early in the training program. Details can be found in Steps One and Two of the training program.

During the fourth stage you will be shown how to provide your brain with positive mental programs while it is in a highly receptive condition. As with the other skills, this is not a particularly difficult procedure to master although it does require an investment of time and effort in order to practise.

The fifth and final stage is to put your new approach to work in real-life situations.

Before we start working on the practical procedures however, I should like to set the scene by explaining how and why the Alpha Plan can have such a powerful and positive effect on performance.

TWO
Brain Waves

*'Learning to control brain-wave patterns . . . does
not depend on normal sensory feedback, but on the
development of awareness of subtle, internal
sensations that normally we do not notice . . .
through the use of this increased awareness we train
our bodies to function more optimally.'*

Elmer and Alyce Green *Beyond Biofeedback*

Visitors to my workshops are often surprised to see
men and women of all ages, and from many professional backgrounds, busy playing with toy trains.
Far from bringing out the child in them, the railway is
being used to help perfect a vital mental skill. They are
learning to control the way their brain works in order to
make it work more effectively.

The train set is simply an intriguing and dramatic way
of demonstrating what is happening inside their minds
and how they can both monitor these processes and
exert voluntary control over them. They are learning to
produce, at will and for an extended period, a type of
electrical activity called alpha waves. Subjectively the
alpha state is one of relaxed alertness. Technically it
refers to electrical activity with a frequency of between
about 8 and 14 cycles per second (see Fig. 1). The more
alpha is produced the faster the train runs around its
track. Sometimes there are contests to see who can
complete the circuit in the shortest time.

Since many of those attending Alpha-Plan workshops are competitive business executives, they quickly
warm to the challenge and feel confident of doing well.
But this is a very paradoxical race, since the more you
want to win the less likely you are to do so. In this
contest the conventional high achiever usually comes
last. One of the first lessons to learn is that alpha
production is a business where you succeed *only* by not
really trying.

When first wired up to the monitoring equipment

FIG. 1

Mains electricity is supplied to houses in the UK at 50
cycles per second, in the USA at 60 cycles, per second.
This means that the voltage goes through 50 or 60 cycles,
like the one shown below, every second. The term *hertz*,
abbreviated to Hz, is also used to describe each complete
cycle which represents the frequency of the current.

The highest voltage reached during the cycle is called
the peak voltage. There is both a positive and a negative
peak. The total or peak-to-peak voltage in the graph
below is 240 volts.

The brain and nervous system produce this type of
electrical current, although the voltages are far smaller –
in the order of 0.000050 of a volt rather than the 240 volts
of domestic power.

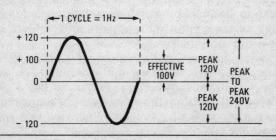

most people generate short bursts of alpha and the train moves falteringly. After a little practice, however, alpha is being generated almost continuously, and the engine speeds along. By producing a different type of brain wave, subjects can bring the train to an immediate halt. Most find it a remarkable and convincing demonstration of their brain's previously unrealised capacity for self-regulation.

Although it may seem to some to be verging on the paranormal, there is nothing in the least supernatural about the process. What happens is that contacts, attached to the scalp, pick up the electrical activity deep within the brain and carry these signals to an extremely sensitive receiving device, known as an electro-encephalogram, or EEG. This detects the electrical activity, filters out unwanted signals – for instance the electricity being generated by the muscles of the jaw and scalp – and then presents the waves in some useful way. An EEG print-out may consist of wavy lines drawn on a moving band of paper, a pulsating tone or a flickering light. Some of the smaller EEGs, used for biofeedback training rather than medical diagnosis, make a noise like rain drumming on to a tin roof. The rhythm of this sound matches the rhythmic currents of the brain's electrical patterns. Other machines have lights which pulse in synchrony with the brain waves. I use a toy train because experience has shown that this type of feedback captures the interest and so increases motivation. Brain training in this way helps people gain mastery of their mind more rapidly and easily than when using other outputs.

But while such electronic devices are a useful aid in training, they are certainly not essential. For the purposes of improving performance using the Alpha Plan what matters is not the generation of specific brain waves but the subjective state of mind associated with those waves.

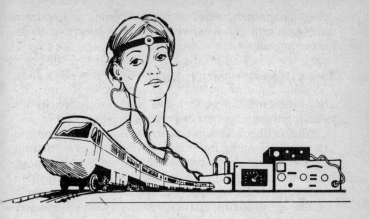

This can be achieved without any assistance from costly and complicated gadgets. All it takes is the right training and a desire to practise and acquire this important skill. It involves developing the ability to monitor and control very subtle mental sensations which are quite unlike the feelings which arise from any other part of the body. The ways in which these skills can be acquired are explained in Step Two of the training program.

American biofeedback experts Elmer and Alyce Green, of the Menninger Foundation, have expressed the process as follows:

> Brain-wave patterns have no sensory concomitants – that is, there are no sensory processes by means of which we can detect the presence of brain-wave activity. We can detect tense muscles, cold hands, or a pounding heart, but there is no way to sense brain-wave activity. What we sense and control is not the brain wave itself, but a state of consciousness, a concatenation of subtle existential cues.

In this chapter I want to say a little about the discovery of alpha and its relationship to other types of brain waves.

The Discovery of Alpha

The flickering flames of cave fires probably gave mankind the earliest experiences of induced alpha production. It's been shown that this type of subtly changing red light markedly influences the brain's electrical activity. During training workshops we sometimes mimic this effect by means of a pulsating strobe lamp. It tends to produce rapid and powerful alpha.

Although electrical activity was detected in the brain as early as the eighteenth century, it was not until 1924 that alpha waves were discovered and named by Hans Berger, a German psychiatrist.

Berger had originally intended to study astronomy, but changed his mind after a near fatal riding accident while serving with the German cavalry. One afternoon, while the nineteen-year-old was exercising his mount, the animal stumbled over an embankment and flung him directly under the thundering hooves of a horse-drawn field gun. Somehow he managed to roll clear and escaped with nothing worse than minor bruises. That evening Berger received a telegram from his father inquiring after his health. Berger senior explained that, at what turned out to be the precise moment of the young man's brush with death, his sister had experienced such a powerful premonition of danger that she insisted that her father telegraph to find out if he was safe. Recalling this incident in 1940 Berger wrote: 'This is a case of spontaneous telepathy in which at a time of mortal danger, and as I contemplated certain death, I transmitted my thoughts, while my sister, who was particularly close to me, acted as the receiver.'

On resuming his studies Berger switched from astronomy to psychiatry in order to explore the link between physical and psychical events. In 1924, after years of research, Berger made the first ever recordings of brain waves through the skull of his fifteen-year-old son Klaus. He identified two types of electrical activity; short-duration waves which he called *beta* and others which were larger, slower, more long-lasting. These he named *alpha* waves.

Berger's career ended tragically when the Nazis hounded him to suicide. But his discoveries established him as one of the key figures in brain research and the rhythmic alpha patterns he first recorded are sometimes referred to as Berger waves.

During the mid-fifties a British researcher, W. Grey Walter, of the Burden Neurological Institute, introduced his toposcope. This provided an instantaneous display of overall brain function on 22 cathode-ray tubes placed in an elliptical array to represent the shape of a patient's head when viewed from above. The advance allowed neurologists to map the timing of waves in different parts of the brain. Grey Walter explained:

> We now know that within the brain, a great many electric processes can be identified, each with its own limited domain, some apparently independent, others interacting with one another. We must accept that in the EEG we are dealing essentially with a symphonic orchestral composition, but one in which the performers may move about a little, and may follow the conductor or indulge in improvisation – more like a jazz combination than a solemn philharmonic assembly.

The Beginning of Brain-training

For many years the EEG was only used for medical diagnosis. By studying the paper charts, neurologists could identify such problems as tumours or epilepsy which left a distinctive spiky wave signature.

Then, in 1958, American psychologist, Joe Kamiya opened up an exciting new field of research and training. While researching into sleep, at the University of Chicago, Kamiya became fascinated 'by the alpha rhythm that came and went in waking EEGs and wondered if, through laboratory experiments with the easily traced rhythm, a subject could be taught awareness of an internal state'.

After wiring volunteers, with no previous training, up to an EEG he placed each alone in a darkened room. Their brains' electrical activity was fed to monitoring equipment in a nearby laboratory. From time to time he sounded a bell in the subjects' rooms and asked them to guess whether or not they were producing alpha. He then told them if that guess was correct or not.

On the first day subjects guessed right only about 50 per cent of the time, a result no better than would be expected from chance alone. By day two, however, their success rate had crept up to 65 per cent and on the third day 85 per cent of guesses were correct. After only four days' training every subject was able to identify the alpha state with complete accuracy in 400 separate trials. Kamiya's research clearly demonstrated that people were 'able to control their minds to the extent of entering and sustaining either state upon command'.

As more and more men and women were given the chance to train their brains to produce alpha, interesting findings emerged about those who proved especially adept at the task. Kamyia reported that they were very agreeable people to work with: 'I generally tend to have more positive liking for the individual who sub-

sequently turns out to learn alpha control more readily,'
he commented.

The Experience of Alpha

Alpha is generally associated with feelings of relaxed
awareness. The mind is tranquil yet receptive. These
brain waves are also associated with pleasurable and
rewarding activities. During the sixties, electrical
activity in the brains of American footballers was
monitored, by means of portable EEGs and miniature
radio transmitters, during actual matches. Alpha highs
were consistently recorded immediately after a successful touchdown.

It has also been found that people with well-defined
alpha waves have greater aptitide for meditation and
may show extrasensory powers. The late C. Maxwell
Cade, an eminent British researcher, identified what he
termed a 'dowsing' alpha: short bursts of low voltage
waves, which appear approximately half a second
before the dowsing reaction occurs. He reported:

> When asked to stand still with eyes closed the
> dowser showed the usual high level of alpha from
> both hemispheres. As he began to walk with eyes
> closed over the same ground, this steady alpha
> was replaced by alpha bursts, such that it was
> impossible to say from the EEG whether his eyes
> were open or closed. Presumably as soon as the
> dowser gave his attention to walking, the alpha
> from the occipital lobe[1] 'blocked' whereas the
> dowsing alpha appears from a different area of the
> brain.

People who have learned meditation, yoga or a

[1] Area at back of the brain concerned with vision.

similar mind-centring discipline and those with healing powers typically produce the most alpha and can usually do so with the least difficulty. But such self-regulation is a natural talent everybody possesses and can develop with practice.

Brain Waves

So far I have considered only alpha waves, with a frequency of between around 8 and 14 cycles per second (Hz). But, as Fig. 2 shows, the brain generates many other forms of electrical activity depending on one's mood, activity and circumstances.

Beta is associated with active thinking, paying attention, focusing on the outside world and solving complex problems. However, the relationship between mental activity and electrical activity is not quite as simple as this. If asked to perform some simple calculation, such as 143 minus 67, most people will show increased beta production. Yet when people are asked to find the square roots of numbers, in their heads, they tend to produce more alpha.

A possible explanation is that we all know how to do subtraction, but have forgotten how to find square roots. In searching back to school lessons for the procedure needed, the cortex remains relatively inactive and this allows alpha to appear. A professional mathematician, who immediately knew how to find square roots, would be more likely to produce beta. Yet, interestingly, some great thinkers – Albert Einstein was one of them – have been shown to solve complex problems while producing mainly alpha.

Around 10 per cent of the normal population produce almost continuous beta and very little alpha, even with their eyes closed. This may be due to elevated anxiety levels, but could also be caused by having extremely alert and active brains.

Fig. 2 Brain Waves

Name	Frequency	Characteristics
Delta	0.5–4.0	Deep sleep
Theta	5.0–7.0	Twilight sleep, between waking and sleeping. Also present at moments of insight or when recalling a vivid memory
Alpha	8.0–14	Relaxed alertness. Brain not working on any specific task, or engaged on a routine activity. Receptive. Most easily achieved with eyes closed
Beta	15–22	Alert, concentrating on demanding task. Anxious or apprehensive
High Beta	23–35	Brain very active. Thinking hard about a complex problem or during anxiety attacks

Note: Ranges are only approximate and vary between individuals

Theta waves, with a frequency of between 5 and 7 cycles per second, appear mainly in the brain's temporal and parietal regions – that is, approximately halfway between the back and front of the head – and are strongest in the left side. They seem to be associated with emotional states, since children generate them especially when laughing or crying. In adults the ending of a pleasant activity also increases theta output. As with alpha, the brain shows higher levels of theta production when the eyes are closed, and appears most strongly as consciousness slips towards drowsiness.

During this stage of what the English poet and psychical researcher Frederick Myers called hypnagogic sleep (from the Greek *hypnos*, 'sleep', plus *agogos*, 'leading') the mind is often filled with powerful images. Unlike day-dreams, these appear to be the projection of impulses from sources below the levels of normal awareness. Myers used the term hypnopompic images to describe the very similar scenes which, appearing as if from nowhere as we wake up again the next morning, are often surprising and even startling.

As sleep overtakes us, theta gives way to delta waves, the slowest oscillations found, with frequencies as low as 0.5 cycles per second. Delta waves dominate the EEGs of children up to the age of twelve months.

Grey Walter, emphasising their protective function, compared delta waves to the 'dead man's handle' on a train.

> During delta activity no useful work can be done by the neurons concerned. Sometimes the delta waves are so large that we may suspect them of paralysing the cortex by electrocution, as it were, and we may speculate as to whether this may not be their special function in certain conditions, just as the function of pain is sometimes to immobilise an injured part.

A similar effect is found in many sleeping animals, and has the effect of 'disengaging' brain and body, just as the 'dead man's handle' on a train cuts off power should the driver fall asleep or be taken ill.

By preventing the muscles from obeying the very vigorous commands from the sleeping brain, animals and humans avoid harming themselves – and others – during rest. For example, if a man has a vivid dream of strangling his partner, the delta-wave paralysis of the brain serves to stop the fantasy being translated into an actual murder.

Studies of the brain waves of many hundreds of children and young people, ranging in age from 3 months to 19 years, enabled Charles E. Henry of Western Reserve University School of Medicine to plot the changes in wave patterns across time.

At around 3 to 4 months, the most frequently observed are slow delta waves, reflecting the infant's long periods of sleep. By 12 months the waves have increased in frequency to between 5 and 6 cycles (theta waves) per second. From 2 to 5 years, these theta waves continue to be the dominant electrical activity, but after the age of 5, alpha waves start appearing until they are equal to theta. As the child grows into his teens, theta gradually declines while alpha increases, and beta starts making an appearance. Without special training to recapture the relaxed alertness which characterises the mental state of most young children, adults, as we have seen, usually produce more beta than alpha.

The Alpha Plan

During Step Two of the training programme described in this book, you will learn how to increase alpha production in order to achieve a frame of mind most sensitive to receiving fresh commands.

But, as with the physical relaxation procedures taught in Step One, knowing how to control alpha will enhance your life in many other ways as well. By increasing inner tranquillity it helps safeguard you against life's stresses. By freeing the brain from the burden of needless worries, it assists intellectual functioning. Solving problems and making decisions is far easier when you are no longer distracted by petty concerns. In alpha – that is, the state of being when the brain is producing alpha waves – the mind is usually more creative and imaginative than in beta. The training also assists emotionally by reducing the power of those negative thoughts that produce anxiety and depression.

After only a few practice sessions you should start feeling, and appearing, calmer, more relaxed and more in control of your inner self and your outer life.

THREE
Your Biocomputer Brain

'More and more, as the brain yields its secrets to research, it is possible to see its inner workings without mystery and to realise that it performs as a machine, albeit a very complicated one.'

Dr R. J. Stevens *Computer versus Brain*

The danger of comparing the workings of the mind to the functioning of a computer is that it can easily lead to an overly simplistic view of how the brain works, replacing white rats by microchips in an effort to explain the complexities of human thought. As Dr Michael Arbib of the University of Massachusetts rightly cautions, 'We must stay alive to the fact that human action, memory, learning, and perception are far richer than those of any machine yet built or likely to be built in the near future.' That said, the metaphor can still help us both to understand mental functioning better and, even more importantly from a practical point of view, to enhance its performance.

Our brain represents a supreme survival success story. Out of the countless trillions of alternatives which have occurred during some 500 million years of evolution, this structure has emerged as the one best suited to meeting the challenges of nature and the demands of human society.

With 2 million visual, and 100,000 acoustic, inputs, an estimated 13 billion neurons and 70 billion glial cells –

the supporting structure of nervous tissue – the human brain is a biological computer in continuous operation and capable of performing millions of parallel computations simultaneously. It represents the most highly organised structure in the known universe.

Put simply, the grapefruit-sized lump of organic matter nestling between your ears, and currently interpreting the printed symbols on this page, is a mechanical marvel beyond technology's wildest dreams.

Even more encouragingly, for those who doubt the quality of their brains, independent studies at the University of Oregon Medical School, Columbia University and Ohio State University, have concluded that there is little structural difference between the mental apparatus of averagely bright people and that of such great geniuses as Isaac Newton and Albert Einstein.

Yet the sad truth is that only a tiny minority of the billions of humans who have inhabited this planet in the millennia since our species first formed societies can be considered geniuses; some believe that less than fifty men and women truly deserve that title. Sadder yet, a mere 2 per cent of the present-day populations of Europe and America have an IQ high enough even to be considered 'very bright'.

Research by Professor Warren McCulloch and his colleagues at the Massachusetts Institute of Technology has revealed an almost criminal waste of human intellectual potential. They report that even people with an IQ of 180 – genius level – use less than a third of their total mental capacity. Most people probably make use of less than a quarter.

Something has obviously gone badly wrong! If, as studies suggest, our mental powers are vastly superior to those of the most advanced computer, why do so many of us have difficulty in tackling mundane tasks which ought to be performed easily and effortlessly?

To understand the true reason for failure we need to explore more closely this analogy between brain and computer.

The Hardware In Your Head

Take the lid off a computer and you'll find its hardware, the microchips (more properly called integrated circuits or ICs), printed circuit boards, data transfer lines (buses), power transformer, resistors and other components which make up the machine's physical presence.

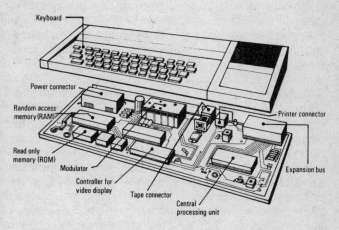

Slice the top off a human skull, cut through the layers of protective membrane, the meninges, and you'll find the brain's hardware, some 1,450 grams of deeply convoluted, pinkish-grey matter partially divided into two cerebral hemispheres.

When examined under a microscope an IC reveals a dense complexity of transistors, diodes, capacitors and other circuit elements so tightly packed together on the 6 × 6 mm piece of silicon that even with high-power

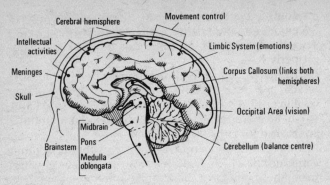

magnification it is impossible to distinguish between them.

Replace the silicon chip with a sliver of cerebral cortex and an even greater complexity is found, with around 10,500 neurons per cubic millimetre. Each is equivalent in power to the average home computer.

Parts of the cerebral cortex appear grey, others look white due to the presence of myelin, an insulating material which helps to speed impulses along the nerve. These impulses, purely electrical in the computer but both electrical and chemical in the brain, are, literally, both the messengers of thought and the thoughts themselves. Without them neither machine nor mind can function.

The working brain is such a frenetic hub of electro-chemical activity that the great pioneer neurologist Sir Charles Sherrington likened it to 'an enchanted loom where flashing shuttles weave a dissolving pattern: always a meaningful pattern but never an abiding one.'

If you were small enough to enter the human skull and stand on the surface of a human brain, the polyneural roar produced by these impulses would be as deafening as a city-centre rush-hour. Not surprisingly, neither the electrical signal in a computer nor the neural impulses in the nervous system move around at random. Indeed any that do so are termed 'noise' by engineers and, if there is too much noise in the system then neither machine nor mind can function properly.

This happens in the human body when, for reasons which are not yet fully understood, the insulating myelin sheath breaks down, causing impulses to short-circuit and producing the crippling disease of multiple sclerosis.

In an efficiently functioning system the direction of these impulses is controlled both by the hardware – how the mental or electronic apparatus has been put together – and by the software – those instructions, or programs, which direct and regulate its performance.

The Software In Your Skull

To understand the role of software in the operation of both computers and brains, consider three students who are each given a pocket calculator and told to calculate how far a ship's lookout sees from the top of a seventy-foot mast.

There is a simple formula for working out the distance, in miles, from any height above sea level, to the horizon. You multiply the height in feet by 3, divide the result by 2 and then take the square root. To solve the problem above, therefore, we simply multiply 70 by 3, to give 210; divide by 2, which equals 105 and find the square root, producing an answer of 10.25 miles.

Suppose one student quickly arrives at the right answer, the second gives the correct solution but takes twice as long, while the third announces that the distance is 1633 miles. How can these differences be explained?

We might argue that only one of the calculators is working properly: that used by the fast, accurate

student. The second performs accurately but slowly, while the third is a complete dud. We could also suggest that the faulty calculators must have been poorly designed, badly made or damaged in transit. Perhaps all three. We'll call this explanation the dud-calculator theory.

However, although not impossible, it is unlikely to be the first explanation which comes to mind. More probably we will assume that the successful student used his calculator quickly and correctly, the second slowly but correctly, while the third either pushed the right buttons in the wrong sequence or the wrong ones entirely.

If we reasoned in this way we have chosen the faulty-use theory in preference to the dud-calculator theory to explain their differing degrees of success. Rather than blaming the designer, the manufacturer or the shop-keeper for incompetence we search for explanations in terms of the instructions given to those machines. This may sound so obvious that it appears to be no more than the application of sound common sense. Yet, remarkably, when asked to explain variations in human intellectual performance there are many who strongly advocate the equivalent of the dud-calculator theory while insisting that the faulty-use theory has little or no relevance.

They argue that clever people have good brains; those of average intelligence have fairly good brains; while stupidity is caused by bad brains. Furthermore, they propose that the quality of construction is mainly – if not exclusively – determined by heredity. Good genes produce good brains, while poor genes result in sub-standard thinking apparatus. Thus we are all, in a sense, victims or victors in a game of genetic roulette, being born bright or dumb and remaining in that state from the womb to the tomb.

As with the theory of the dud calculators, a malfunc-tion of the hardware may be attributed to a design fault, manufacturer's error, damage in transit or any com-bination of the three.

Now some brains do, of course, have design faults due to errors in the genetic blueprint responsible for their construction. Perhaps the most common of these is the mental retardation associated with Down's syn-drome. This leads to a smaller than average brain with widespread defects in the cell layers responsible for the highest levels of thought. There may also be a 'construc-tion' failure, which happens when the infant is starved during the critical, early, months of mental develop-ment. Protein-energy malnutrition (PEM), leading to the clinical condition known as kwashiorkor, causes a reduction in the growth of brain tissue and severe, long-term impairment of general reasoning ability. Finally, a failure to function efficiently may be due to physical damage resulting from accident or deliberately inflicted injury.

It should be noted, however, that even in cases of fairly severe brain damage, the mental hardware is often capable of functioning at a far higher level than many people either realise or may be willing to recognise. Work by American therapist Glenn Doman and his colleagues, at the Institutes for the Achievement of Human Potential, has shown that, with the appropriate therapies, a significant proportion of severely brain-damaged youngsters can be helped to live a more normal life.

Similarly studies by Dr John Lorber of the Children's Hospital in Sheffield have provided remarkable evidence for the high level of performance which can often be achieved by even profoundly brain-damaged individuals. He has been looking at the achievements of children suffering from hydrocephalus, or 'water on the brain' which is due to a build-up of fluid in the brain compressing the grey matter of the cerebral hemispheres. On occasions this compression is so great that a beam of light placed one side of the skull is seen as a red glow from the opposite side. One might imagine that such children would be so severely brain-damaged as to be incapable of even the simplest mental feat. Yet, in many cases, the greatly reduced brain continues to function at a high level. The IQ of one young male sufferer, studied by Dr Lorber, was 136 and he had an honours degree in economics.

After a lifetime of working with brain-damaged children, Glenn Doman poses the vital question: 'How long could we look at Johnny, who had half his brain removed, and see him perform as well as Billy, who had an intact brain, without asking the question what is wrong with Billy? Why did not Billy, who had twice as much brain as Johnny, perform twice as well . . .?'

The answer to this all-important question lies not in the hardware but in the software: those sets of instructions which the brain uses to perform its multiplicity of functions. These are the programs in the brain which, having been created by our experiences in life, then shape future experiences and, in doing so, control our behaviour and determine our destiny.

It is with these programs, their evaluation, modification and enhancement, that the Alpha Plan is concerned.

FOUR
Brainware

> '*I propose to say that the lives of human beings, and
> other animals, are governed by sets of programs
> written in their genes and brains.*'
>
> J. Z. Young *Programs of the Brain*

The idea that the human brain operates through the use of 'programs' may, perhaps, be new to you. Yet it has become an increasingly accepted idea among neurologists, cognitive psychologists and researchers in the rapidly developing study of artificial intelligence.

In this book *Programs of the Brain*, the eminent British neuro-anatomist Professor J. Z. Young explains that

> some of the programs may be called 'practical' or physiological and they ensure that we breathe, eat, drink and sleep. Others are social, and regulate our speaking or other forms of communication. Perhaps the most important programs of all are those used for the activities we call mental, such as thinking, imagining, dreaming and believing.

Technically a program is defined as 'a set of instructions arranged in proper sequence for directing the computer to perform a desired operation', in other words for getting it to do what we want.

People who write computer programs have a saying:

Garbage In – Garbage Out – or GIGO. This emphasises the crucial fact that the computer's output reflects its software. When the human brain runs garbage programs – and we all possess a great many of these – our thoughts, words and deeds must inevitably be intellectual, emotional or physical garbage. And that implies a failure to fulfil our true potential: an inability to achieve the goals we set ourselves in life, to express ourselves clearly, to remember and recall important facts, to find solutions, make the best possible choices, play a sport to the best of our ability and so on.

Fortunately we have the capacity to replace inadequate programs with fast, efficient ones or modify those which are basically satisfactory but would benefit from some minor improvements, at any moment in life. Changing or modifying programs is possible because, except for a few 'hard-wired' into the brain before birth as part of our evolutionary adaptation to the environment, all are acquired through learning.

When the French novelist Gustave Flaubert remarked that 'everything in life, from talking to dying, must be learned' he was stating a profound but seldom appreciated truth. Attitudes, abilities and achievements, all the knowledge and skills we possess, represent the results of countless lessons, formal and informal, in the schoolrooms of childhood and the classrooms of life. In short we are what we learn.

We are our programs.

Exploring Your Brainware

Before you read any further, I'd like you to get a feel for analysing one of your own programs by attempting to solve the problem on the next page.

It will – hopefully – be unfamiliar to you, which means that your brain will have to create a new program

– by adapting some which are already in your memory –
in order to come up with the right answer.

You may like to know than an average twelve-year-old can solve the problem in around fifteen seconds. I suggest, therefore, that you allow yourself no more than this when working out the solution.

The Problem

Alec is discussing his taste in detective fiction with his friend Martin who wants to buy him a book for his birthday. Instead of telling him which writer he most admires, Alec creates something of a mystery himself by providing the list below.

When you are ready to begin the problem, read through Alec's list. Remember, give yourself just fifteen seconds to work out the answer.

I like Ellery Queen less than Agatha Christie.
I dislike Raymond Chandler less than Dashiell Hammett.
I don't enjoy Conan Doyle as much as Ellery Queen.
I dislike Raymond Chandler more than Conan Doyle.

Which author does Alec like the *least*?

How did you get on?

If you found an answer, how confident are you that your answer is correct?

Before I give you the solution, and explain how brain-teasers like this – they are known as transitive inference problems – can be solved without any effort, I want you to spend a few moments thinking both about how you attempted to find an answer and your feelings towards that problem while you sought a solution, by making an analysis chart. Make two headings: ACTIONS and ATTITUDES.

Under the ACTIONS heading, write a brief description

of the way you set about trying to solve the problem. Did you work with words, repeating the various authors to yourself while trying to rank them in order, or did you rely on images – picturing Ellery Queen, Hercule Poirot, Philip Marlowe, Sam Spade and Sherlock Holmes in your mind as you sought your answer?

Now try and recall any other thoughts in your mind. Did you feel that the task was easy and enjoyable or was your immediate response that you dislike all such challenges? Did you find yourself becoming confused and impatient? Did you tell yourself things like 'I don't have a head for this kind of riddle' or 'I'm not even going to try and work out the answer.' Note these under the ATTITUDES heading on your Analysis Chart.

A Program for Finding the Answer

The correct answer is that Alec likes the author Dashiell Hammet *least* (apologies to all Hammett fans on his behalf!).

There are a number of brainware programs which provide the answer to transitive inference problems, but here is one of the fastest and most reliable.

Start by reading the first line of the problem opposite and asking yourself: 'If all the information I had about the problem was contained in that first line then what would my answer be?' This makes Ellery Queen Alec's least favourite out of the first two authors, so we store Ellery Queen in a memory slot labelled 'Provisional Solution'.

The next step is to glance at the second line to see if there is any fresh information which would lead to a change in that provisional answer. Since Ellery Queen is not mentioned, we can ignore that line of the problem – for the time being – and pass on to the third line.

Here we find that Alec enjoys Conan Doyle less than

Ellery Queen. This means that we forget Ellery Queen and replace Conan Doyle in the 'Provisional Answer' slot.

The final line of the problem tells us that Alec dislikes Raymond Chandler more than Conan Doyle, so another change in provisional answer is called for. Is Raymond Chandler Alec's least-liked author?

If that was your answer you fell into the trap of not returning to the second line of the problem.

Although this made no difference to our solution when the provisional answer was Ellery Queen, it does change the new answer of Raymond Chandler, since it informs us that Alec dislikes Chandler less than Dashiell Hammett.

Unfortunately a lot of words are needed to describe what is, in fact, an extremely fast and effective brainware program for transitive inference problems. Prove this yourself by discovering Alec's favourite detective writer. (The answer is at the end of this chapter.) You should be able to solve the problem in no more than the time it takes you to glance through it.

That last statement is true. My earlier suggestion that the problem could be solved in fifteen seconds by the average twelve-year-old was a lie. Certainly, given the program I've just described, they would have no difficulty in doing so. But without the program most youngsters, like the vast majority of adults, have considerable difficulty in finding a solution in 15 minutes, let alone 15 seconds. Try it yourself on your friends and see how they get on. It's a tricky problem mainly because it is so unfamiliar, which means that there are no programs available for finding the right answer.

So why did I make out that it was child's play? First of all to increase the psychological pressure by leading you to believe that a failure to find the right answer must mean you aren't as smart as a twelve-year-old. Secondly, to place you under a time pressure, because working against the clock is stressful and frequently impairs performance.

When I present this problem to people attending my workshops I further add to their anxiety by saying that one of them will be chosen at random and asked to present her, or his, answer to the rest of the group. I add that the group will be expected to 'punish' any error by jeering, laughing, sarcastic comments and other remarks designed to make the person feel about an inch tall.

Why pile on the agony? Because we often have to solve problems, make decisions, learn new skills, acquire unfamiliar knowledge, or perform complex tasks under exactly these circumstances. It's an anxiety arousing challenge which usually starts in school. 'What's the answer, John?' the teacher demands. John, who knew exactly what to reply a few moments before suddenly finds his mind a complete blank. The teacher frowns with irritation, the rest of the class giggle; John's humiliation is total.

In his book *How Children Fail*, the American teacher and author John Holt explains that adults destroy much of children's intellectual and creative capacity by the things they do to them or make them do:

We destroy this capacity above all by making them afraid: afraid of not doing what other people want, of not pleasing, of making mistakes, of failing, of being *wrong*. Thus we make them afraid to gamble, afraid to experiment, afraid to try the difficult and the unknown . . . we use these fears as handles to manipulate them and get them to do what we want . . . we find ideal the kind of 'good' children who are just enough afraid of us to do everything we want, without making us feel that fear of us is what is making them do it.

Such experiences are not, of course, confined to

school. Learner-drivers who performed faultlessly on their last lesson crumble into quivering failures during the test itself. Job-hunters who are well qualified and confident become tongue-tied and incapable of answering even the simplest question during interviews. Capable and hardworking students suddenly forget all they have so carefully studied the second they open their exam papers. Professional sportsmen disappoint their fans by coming apart under the pressure of a big match.

From asking for a first date to making a speech, from asserting oneself in a family row to coping with a phobia – the list of situations in which negative thoughts can undermine, or even completely prevent, successful performance is virtually unending. We know how to do what we want to do, but just don't seem able to do it.

If you look at your list of the feelings in your mind when attempting to solve the problem you may well find that some negative, performance-diminishing, thoughts have been noted down. If, on the other hand, you felt that the task was easy your thoughts were likely to have been along the lines of 'piece of cake', 'the answer is obvious', 'only a fool would have difficulty with this'.

Where the answer was right and not arrived at through a lucky guess, those thoughts were clearly realistic. When the answer was wrong, such unrealistic attitudes were as unhelpful to efficient thinking as the more obviously negative notions.

The two columns on that chart also illustrate important differences between how a computer works and how the human brain operates.

First, even the most efficient modern computer operates like a supermarket with a single check-out point. The most sophisticated programs have to be followed one step at a time.[1] The human brain breaks out of this

[1] This will not, however, be the case of Fifth Generation computers whose processing will also be parallel.

bottle-neck by using parallel-processing, which involves putting billions of neurons to work simultaneously. We can converse as we drive to work, and digest our lunch as we think.

A second major difference lies in our ability to experience emotions. AI specialist Dr Jerre Levy comments:

> I know of no artificial-intelligence program that incorporates joy and grief, love and hate, hope and wonder – all the motivations, drives, values, and purposes that are integrated with and condition what and how we perceive, think and choose. I doubt that it is possible for a computer program to model these, because this integration, this complexity, this intimate connection between emotion, cognition, and purposes derives from a brain whose organisational properties represent eons of evolution that has set not only what can be called the hard-wired neurological patterns but the rules by which experience is incorporated into the brain's operation.

Parallel-processing means that when faced with any activity the brain runs not one sort of program but two. First there are programs which are concerned with the *how* aspects of performance. They tell us *how* to perform such tasks as driving a car, playing the piano, spelling a word, solving a mathematical problem, making a decision, hitting a tennis ball and so on. Because the end result is frequently, although not invariably, an activity of some type we can refer to them as action programs.

But the brain also has programs which determine *when* and *where* and *why* action programs are used. These we may conveniently call management programs.

To picture the relationships between Action and

Management programs, think of them as units of some vast company.

As the illustration shows, this organisation owns factories where they make a wide range of different goods and manages them through offices at local, branch, divisional and national level. In overall command is the international board of directors who take decisions affecting every part of the group. The factories and offices keep in touch with one another by telephone and telex lines, through computer links, the mail and regular meetings.

The company's performance depends on three closely related factors:

1. The efficiency of the factories, the skill of the workers, the quality of the tools they are given, an

uninterrupted supply of raw materials and so on.

2. The efficiency of the management at all its various levels, from the shop-floor foreman right up to the board of directors.

3. The efficiency of communications between the two. Are the managers kept informed, clearly and objectively, of everything going on on the shop floor? Are the workers fully aware of the expectations of management?

A failure in any of these three components will, obviously, result in the company working below its full potential and, if the mistakes are profound enough and repeated sufficiently frequently, could result in a complete breakdown of production.

Your success or failure in life depends, similarly, on the efficient functioning of three related elements:

1. The efficiency of your *action programs*.
2. The efficiency of your *management programs*.
3. The effectiveness of *communications* between the two.

In the next chapter I shall be describing the relationship between management and action programs in more detail and we will be considering how information can become seriously distorted when flowing between the two.

A lot of important ground has been covered in these early chapters, so before moving on it may be helpful to summarise the key points discussed.

Summary

I have likened the brain to a computer and drawn a distinction between hardware (microchips, resistors and other components in the machine, neurons and synapses in the brain) and software: that is, the programs which computer and brain run in order to perform some task.

The better your brainware, the more efficiently and successfully you perform. A failure to succeed is far more frequently the result of a software failing than a hardware fault.

But because programs, both action and management, are acquired through learning, new ones can be established and earlier ones modified throughout life. The easiest way to do this is to place mind and body in the highly receptive state associated with high-level alpha production.

The Alpha Plan shows you how to bring about these essential changes as quickly, as easily and as effortlessly as possible.

Alec's favourite detective writer is Agatha Christie.

FIVE
How Brainware is Built

*'When we suggest that the brain can be thought of
in some ways as a programmed computer, we are
not trying to reduce humans to the level of extant
machines, but rather to understand ways in which
machines can give us insight into human attributes.'*

Michael A. Arbib *The Metaphorical Brain*

Martin wants to speak better German in order to get a
job abroad; Sarah needs a clearer understanding of
statistics if she is to pass her exams; Alison hopes for a
place in her club's squash team.

Three very different goals but all approached in the
same way – by practising. Martin brushes up his German at evening class, Sarah sees her tutor for additional
coaching, Alison spends every free evening at the
courts.

Whenever we seek to achieve some goal, understand
a complex subject, or perfect a demanding sport our
usual strategy is to practise. In other words we seek to
enhance our Action Programs.

Sometimes this proves perfectly satisfactory. But
there will be many other occasions when, no matter
how much time, effort and energy we invest in trying to
master new skills or perfect old ones, more practice
makes little or no difference. Indeed it may seem that
the harder we try to improve our action programs the
worse we perform. Consider, for example, the fear and

loathing which number problems arouse in so many people. Despite having spent hundreds of hours in school attempting to acquire action programs for solving various sorts of sums they remain apparently incapable of tackling even simple calculations.

To understand why this happens, and how we can best prevent such failures in the future, we need to consider both how action programs are acquired and the way management programs regulate our ability to carry them out.

Action Programs

The graph below illustrates how new action programs are acquired.

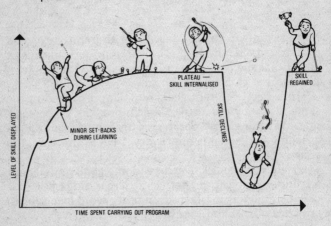

As the initially steep slope of the line indicates, progress is usually rapid when we first set out to acquire a new action program. In just a short time many basic features of the skill have been mastered. As an example, think of the way we learn to drive a car. In their first few lessons, most learners get a chance to try out the majority of the action programs they will ever use when motoring. From never having sat behind the wheel of a car before, a learner may find it reasonably easy to start the engine, shift into gear, move away from the kerb, steer around obstacles and stop again. But subsequent progress, as these basic skills are refined, is usually a great deal slower. This is shown by the way the learning curve flattens out towards the top.

While learning there are bound to be occasions when performance declines for no apparent reason and we wonder miserably why on earth we ever thought we would be able to succeed in such a complicated activity. These temporary set-backs are indicated by the small indentations in an otherwise smoothly curving line.

Eventually we will have perfected the action programs as fully as we can hope to using those particular training methods, although it might still be possible to improve further if different skills were taught. For instance, having passed his or her test the motorist might decide to take an advanced motoring course, or to learn to drive a racing car.

This point, at which the skill is said to be *internalised*, is shown by the flat 'plateau' on the drawing. Having reached it we are able to carry out the activity more or less automatically. An experienced driver can motor safely and effortlessly through even heavy traffic while thinking about other things.

If we stop practising for a while our skill will decline, as shown by the abrupt dip in the curve, but it will never be lost entirely and may be recovered with much less effort and in a far shorter period of time than was needed to master it originally. An adult who learned to ride a bicycle aged six will still be able to do so sixty years later, even though he hasn't done so for more than half a century. A little practice is all that's necessary to regain his former proficiency, the action program being re-established with far less time and effort than it took to learn in the first place.

Management Programs

But having an action program that allows us to do something does not mean we will either want or need to use it. For instance, we know not only how to take our clothes off, but also where, when and why it is appropriate to do so.

These management programs were acquired during early childhood at the same time that we learned to undress. Their precise nature will, however, be determined by parental attitudes towards nudity; if our parents were very modest we might feel far more inhibited about undressing than had they been naturists. So while similar action programs will be found among individuals belonging to the same social or cultural groups, the management programs which regulate them are often far more idiosyncratic.

Management programs are acquired from the earliest days of infancy onwards as we discover, slowly and sometimes painfully, how the world works. The infant constantly dropping her rattle out of the cot is like a scientist performing an experiment. She is finding out what happens when a particular action is performed, and the results will teach her many important lessons. First, she will come to understand that it is possible to co-ordinate hand and eye movements in order to achieve a chosen goal. Secondly, she will discover that if one lets go of something it drops downwards. Thirdly, she learns that things make different noises when they reach the ground – the rattle thuds, teddy thumps, a rice pudding slurps and so on. Fourthly, she learns that grown-ups respond to this activity in various ways, which teaches her that it is possible to exert control over other people's behaviour.

The type of management programs which develop as a result of using the 'dropping things' action program, will depend on the response which she gets from her parents and others. If Mummy is always cross and Daddy is comforting, one of these programs may tell her: 'Don't drop the rattle when Mum is around, wait for Dad to come home.' If both parents get angry when it's rice pudding rather than a rattle which is being flung to the floor, the management program may tell her: 'Don't drop rice puddings when adults are around.'

The interaction of these action and management programs generates higher-level management programs whose spheres of influence are much greater and whose significance is far more profound. In the example above, the infant who finds Mummy punishing and Daddy indulgent when it comes to dropping things may draw a more general conclusion about the amount of love felt for her by either parent. This program will, quite clearly, control a much wider range of behaviours, since it influences everything the child does which is related to her parents.

Even more significantly, the child may draw general conclusions about the nature of all women and all men as a result of these early experiences. During adolescence and adulthood, long after she has forgotten all about dropping toys and food, she may find herself relating more warmly to men than to women, and perhaps become anxious in the presence of older women, especially those who appear most like her mother. It may also make her wary of carrying out 'experiments' which are disapproved of by her parents. She may come to feel that any behaviour which is out of the ordinary, or different, is bad and should be avoided. Such a management program will, of course, greatly inhibit creativity and risk-taking, while encouraging conventional thoughts, words and deeds.

In isolating just one aspect of behaviour, 'dropping

things', I have clearly oversimplified what is an enormously complicated series of inter-relationships between our actions and other people's reactions, between our reactions to their reactions, their reactions to our reactions and so on. However, this example does, I hope, illustrate two crucial aspects of brainware. Firstly, there is a close relationship between doing and feeling, between programs that produce action and those that regulate those actions. Secondly, management programs are arranged in a hierarchy, as the illustration shows.

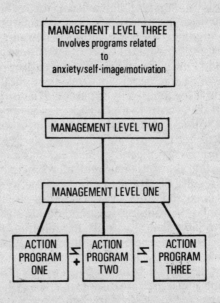

Immediately above the action programs are management programs whose range of influence is fairly limited. These programs are, in turn, regulated by higher-level programs and so on up the hierarchy of command until we arrive at management programs that determine our whole approach to life and form the very core of our being.

The structure is not rigid, however. Lower-level programs can influence or even override those at a higher level under certain circumstances, just as a deputation of shop-floor workers may sometimes persuade senior management to change a policy of which they disapprove.

If you completed the analysis chart (page 46) the notes you kept under the *attitude* heading represent some of the management programs brought to bear on the task of deciding which fictional detective Alec liked least. The same approach can, of course, be applied to any task and later in the book you will be using just this procedure to discover what management programs you run when confronting mentally or physically demanding challenges.

When Martin, a 32-year-old company executive kept records of his management programs over a number of routine activities at work, his analysis form included the following:

Analysis Chart	
Actions	*Attitudes*
Making an important decision	Concerned that I may make a mistake and be seen to fail
Presenting ideas to clients	Frustrated by lack of control over decisions taken
Reviewing documents in presence of superior while problem-solving.	Tense, unable to pay full attention to the material

As you will realise, all Martin's attitudes, or management programs as I shall call them from now on, are likely to exert their influence over a wider range of actions than he noted on the chart. For example, the program which instructed him to become tense when reading in the presence of a superior, could also increase tension in any situation where he was under critical scrutiny. The fear of failure indicated by his response to the making of decisions, or the program responsible for generating feelings of frustration in situations where he is unable to exert full control over outcomes, are likely to regulate an even wider range of actions, from the leisure activities he finds most enjoyable to the way he relates to family and friends.

Positive and Negative Programs

As a result of all our experiences in life we develop two sorts of action and management programs. Some are positive in that they help achieve whatever we seek to achieve. Others are negative since they create barriers to accomplishment. But whether the program is positive or negative largely depends on the circumstances in which it is used.

Anger, for instance, is negative when it causes you to lose control and to say or do things which you later regret. But it would be positive if it motivated you to stand up for your legitimate rights rather than allow others to take unfair advantage of you. Similarly, anxiety may be positive, should your life be threatened, but entirely negative if it prevents you from doing your best in a non-hazardous situation.

There are some programs which are, in my experience, always negative, including those responsible for greed, jealousy, envy, hatred and prejudice; just as there are others whose effects are always positive – for example, those concerned with compassion, forgiveness and generosity. But, for the most part, whether or not a particular program is to be judged positive or negative depends on the answer to this question: is that action or attitude helpful or harmful to me in attaining my ambitions in life? If helpful it is positive. If harmful it is negative.

When the brain is running positive action and management programs we perform with maximum efficiency and reach a desired goal on the shortest possible time and with the least expenditure of effort. Negative programs increase the time, effort and energy that has to be invested in any activity. Even when the influence of such programs is only slight, the results can still prove extremely destructive.

Because negative programs cause us to pay more attention to the things we do wrong than those we get right they tend to reinforce one another, creating a destructive downward spiral. At the same time, by influencing the way we anticipate how we are going to act and what outcome is most likely, they generate a

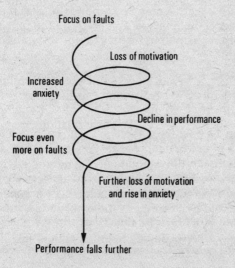

Focus on faults

Loss of motivation

Increased anxiety

Decline in performance

Focus even more on faults

Further loss of motivation and rise in anxiety

Performance falls further

negative feedforward which undermines confidence, increases anxiety and makes failure a more probable outcome than success. This generates a negative program spiral.

Negative spirals produce any, or all, of these feelings:

* Confusion and self-doubt. People trapped in a negative spiral are indecisive and rarely accomplish much.
* Fear and distrust. Such individuals are constantly worried lest they will fail to achieve their goals in life, be cheated by others or denied their rightful rewards.
* Ultracritical views. Disapproval and criticism are the tell-tale signs of people trapped in this negative spiral. There is much more in life that they dislike and do not approve of than they are prepared to like and admire – including, frequently, themselves.

Negative spirals may be so powerful that they exert an influence over virtually everything the person trapped within them does or tries to do. They are likely to result in:

* Failure to achieve one's full potential in life.
* Difficulty in conveying feelings openly and honestly.
* An inability to sustain close relationships.
* Lack of co-operation with others.

Positive program spirals can also be created by focusing on the satisfactory or successful aspects of performance, while reviewing any failures in a constructive manner and by a confident and objective anticipation of the likely outcome of any action.

People with positive program spirals are likely to possess some, or all, of these attributes:

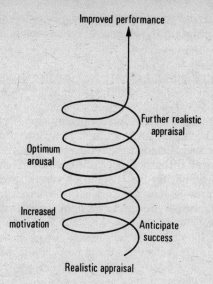

Improved performance

Further realistic appraisal

Optimum arousal

Increased motivation

Anticipate success

Realistic appraisal

* Drive. They are doers as well as thinkers and their investment of effort and energy in all they do is high.
* Confidence. Knowing that they have the ability to succeed in whatever they set their minds to do they approach even tough challenges with assurance and, by so doing, inspire others.
* Calmness. They are quiet and self-possessed, attracting others by the force of their personality.

Positive action and management programs enable goals to be achieved through a relaxed, purposeful drive rather than the investment of excessive effort and energy. By using the creative power of the Alpha Plan to produce positive program spirals, you should find it easier to achieve:

* An attractive personality.

* An ability to co-operate with others and win their co-operation in return. An inner sense of guidance and purpose.
* A zest for living.
* Inspiration and creativity.
* An eagerness to accomplish significant goals in life.

I have explained how programs, mainly acquired through learning, control both the way we behave and the view we take of that behaviour. I have also considered the influence of positive and negative programs. In Chapter Six I shall describe how success or failure may develop into a self-perpetuating system through the twin processes of feedforward and feedback.

SIX

Feedback and Feedforward

*'If we wish to change the sentiments it is necessary
before all to modify the idea which produced them.'*

Paul Dubois

The term feedback, coined by radio pioneers around the turn of the century, has been defined by engineer Norbert Wiener as, 'a method for controlling a system by reinserting into it the results of its past performance'.

The meaning of this rather complicated technical description becomes immediately clear when we consider some everyday examples of feedback in action. Pressure cookers, central heating systems and the human body have one important feature in common: they all maintain themselves within certain limits through the use of feedback.

In the cooker, steam builds up to a certain point at which a valve opens, the vapour is released and the pressure restored to a predetermined level. In a central heating system, a thermostat monitors room temperature, switching the boiler on or off as necessary.

Our body also possesses a great many extremely subtle and sensitive physical feedback systems which are essential to our survival. When a soldier stands at attention for too long he runs the risk of fainting because, without the assistance from the pumping action provided by movements of the leg muscles, the heart is unable to supply enough blood to the brain. The fainting fit is a survival mechanism designed to bring the head down lower in order to improve blood flow and maintain the supply of oxygen to the brain.

A second example of bodily feedback occurs in the regulation of carbon-dioxide levels in the blood. Chemical receptors, located in the arteries of the throat and neck, are constantly monitoring gas levels in the bloodstream and sending this information to the brain's 'respiratory centre'. If carbon-dioxide levels begin to rise, their signals increase in urgency, causing us to breathe more rapidly in an attempt to cleanse the blood of this potentially lethal gas. If you hold your breath too long the respiratory centre has the power to override your conscious wish not to breathe and compel you to take a life-saving breath.

No less sensitive and no less important to our well-being are psychological feedback mechanisms whose function is to help ensure intellectual and emotional balance. To maintain a process of self-maintenance which the American psychologist Walter B. Cannon termed 'homeostasis', or the steady state.

As with bodily functions, homeostasis in action and management programs is achieved through feedback. This occurs both consciously and below the level of normal awareness. We are constantly watching ourselves in action, monitoring the results and modifying our feelings and/or behaviour in the light of these observations.

In addition, we use feedforward to anticipate outcomes and decide which programs are most appropriate for a particular set of circumstances.

Because it is impossible for us to monitor all our behaviour all the time we are obliged to be highly selective in the actions and outcomes to which we attend. To do this we must acquire, once again through learning, a set of programs for regulating not only our actions but the ways in which our brain makes sense of the world.

Programs For Seeing

So far we have only considered output from the biocomputer: that is, the things we say, do and feel as a result of the relationship between action and management programs. But before any behaviour is possible the brain must also receive a constant stream of information from its surroundings. By this I mean both the environment beyond our protective barrier of skin and the interior world of the body.

At every second, from the early weeks of life while it is still secure in the womb, to the moment it dies, the human brain is bombarded by information. After birth the input from our surroundings is via the five senses: sight, hearing, taste, touch and smell. Both before and after birth information from inside the body is transmitted to our brain via a vital, yet seldom recognised, sixth sense.

Within every muscle and joint, for example, are located special sensors (proprioceptors) which, by responding to the movements of the limbs and torso, keep the brain constantly informed of, among other things, the position of our arms and legs in space. If you close your eyes, then attempt to touch the first fingers of each hand with arms fully extended, you'll find that they either make perfect contact or miss by no more than around 1 cm. Without vision to guide us, this is only possible because the signals from muscles allow corrections to be made while the arms are moving towards one another.

Other signals from within arrive at the brain from receptors in the semi-circular canals of the inner ear. These enable us to keep our balance. If a man is blindfolded and a weak electric current is passed across the back of his head, to prevent these signals reaching the brain, he is unable to take more than a few paces without falling.

Confronted by such a bombardment of signals all urgently demanding attention, the brain brings order to impending chaos by strictly limiting the flow of messages allowed through to the regions of higher thought. Systems at lower levels in the brain act, in effect, like the phalanxes of security men, receptionists, secretaries and assistants who protect the peace and privacy of high-status company executives. Each has the power to permit or deny access to the next link in the chain of authority. These filter out information regarded as being of minor significance while allowing any considered to have special relevance to reach the innermost sanctums of conscious thought. This does not mean that the millions of other messengers who demand audience by our brain during every waking moment are necessarily turned away unattended, but that their requirements are dealt with by departments which work largely without reference to, and often unnoticed by, the highest regions of thought.

As you read these words, your brain is running programs – hard-wired into the system rather than acquired through learning – for regulating the routine physical functions of the body: breathing, digesting food, pumping blood and so on. Your brain is also responding automatically to such external signals as temperature changes, noise and light levels, the quality of the air being inhaled and a vast array of other messages without your being aware of them. If anything unexpected should happen – for example, an inexplicable noise from the next room – the guardians of the conscious brain may well decide that this new information is of sufficient importance for consideration at the highest level.

It is also possible consciously to switch attention to a

particular source of information, or to find your attention wandering from one input to the next without your intending that it should do so. While listening to a dull after-dinner speech, for instance, you may well start paying more attention to the sight of an attractive companion, the pressure of the seat under your legs, a whispered conversation from the next table and so on.

One can also switch attention at will. While chatting to a party guest you can listen to her remarks and apparently shut out the babble of other people's conversations. Yet you will almost certainly notice, and respond to, two different signals. The first is a mention of your name anywhere in the room and the second any obscenity!

Learning To See

While all normal babies are born with an ability to see, they are not born with the programs needed for making sense of what is seen. Someone who, blind from birth, has his eyesight restored by surgery in early adulthood will not be able to make sense of the world the moment his bandages are removed. Instead he must slowly and carefully learn to make sense of the visual information now available to his brain. This task is so complex that, quite often, perfect vision is never achieved by such patients. In his book *Eye and Brain*, Richard Gregory describes the unsettling experiences of a 52-year-old man whose sight was restored by means of grafts. He reports:

When the bandages were first removed from his eyes, so that he was no longer blind, he heard the voice of the surgeon. He turned to the voice, and saw nothing but a blur. He realised that this must be a face, because of the voice, but he could not see it. He did not suddenly see the world of objects as we do when we open our eyes.

The popular idea that our senses provide us with a clear and objective view of the world about us is far from correct. What they actually do is supply very limited and partial information from which we construct, and then test out, theories about our surroundings. The subjective nature of visual perception is well illustrated by the ambiguous picture below.

Do you see a young girl or an old woman? People are usually equally divided over this drawing, and will often argue strenuously that their interpretation is correct. One also finds that some people who see it as, say, a young girl find great difficulty in ever seeing it as an old woman, or vice versa.

A second illusion, often used to demonstrate the fact that our perception represents a best guess at what is happening in our surroundings, as opposed to some objective truth, is the cube, shown below.

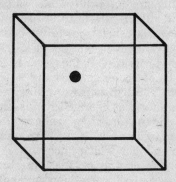

Known as the Necker cube, this illustration offers the brain no clue as to which of several interpretations is correct. It could be, for instance, that the small circle is on the front of the cube, but equally it might be on the rear surface. Faced with this visual ambiguity the brain switches backwards and forwards from one theory about what it is looking at to another, unable to decide which is more likely to be correct since there is no certain evidence either way.

This discussion of the ways in which signals reach the brain, or find the doors closed against them, may seem to have taken us a long way from the role of feedback in establishing and sustaining positive or negative programs. But in fact a knowledge of the processes by which the human biocomputer obtains and uses information is central to an understanding of how programs can be operated.

Imagine that you have moved to a new town and

spend quite a lot of time each day wandering around in order to learn about your new surroundings. The first thing you work out is how to go from your house to the nearest shops. Next you explore the main streets and develop an understanding of how these relate together, and their relationship with important landmarks such as the town square, railway station, public buildings and so on. After a while the central areas and the streets immediately surrounding your house become familiar territory. You can travel, without risk of getting lost, around a large proportion of the town. In time you will also start to be aware of small changes – the fact that somebody has painted their front door red instead of green, that a shop has changed hands, that there are different road signs and so on. Indeed after you have become very familiar with your surroundings it may only be such changes which catch your attention.

All this is possible only because your brain has constructed an internal representation, or mental model, of those streets, roads and buildings. Once this is completed, rather than having to attend to every aspect of our surroundings we can simply pay attention to variations in the environment by comparing incoming information with the mental model. The disadvantage is that we tend to see what we expect to see rather than what may actually be there.

If you read that phrase as 'Paris in the spring', look again. Because that was what you expected to see, that is what your brain told you was actually printed on the page. Seeing what we think should be there rather than taking in data accurately is one of the things which make reading a book for printer's errors so difficult. Both author and editor tend to read the words they expect to find on the page rather than those actually printed there.

Because our environments make such rich and varied information available to us, and because of the ways in which our brain selects out those items of information which seem most relevant to us, it's very unlikely that any two people will see the same surroundings in exactly the same way.

Imagine a policeman, an old lady and an estate agent all walking along the same city street. The policeman is likely to be paying special attention to locks on doors and open skylights; the old lady may be seeing the street through the memories of her chidhood; while the estate agent sees the buildings in terms of their value and possible selling features.

A similar process of selection goes on when we evaluate our own performance. Because we focus on those things which seem most important, and may never even notice anything else, our self-image is bound to exert an important influence on our actual perception.

This selective attention, this focusing on aspects of our surroundings that fit in with the theory we have about ourselves and others, is seen in almost every aspect of life. Indeed an important reason why people have a favourite newspaper is that its particular approach to the selection and interpretation of the news helps to validate their own view of the world. This proves reassuring because it seems to confirm that ours is the 'right' way of looking at life, however unreasonable these views may appear to those who don't share them! As the Austrian psychiatrist Alfred Adler once remarked, 'It is very obvious that we are influenced not by "facts" but by our interpretation of them.'

This seeking out of what appears to us to be the most important information has an unfortunate consequence. It tends to make us gather evidence which confirms a particular management program while discounting, or even failing to notice, any information which might contradict that program.

Suppose you have a management program which makes you feel that you are bad at making speeches. Because of this you become extremely anxious each time you are obliged to do any public speaking. While you are attempting this task, the programs controlling perceptions will be seeking out evidence in support of the management program. If you are addressing 1,000 people, and one person has fallen asleep, then it's very likely that your attention will immediately be drawn to him. Your threshold for this kind of information is much lower than it is for other sights and sounds. Ignoring the 999 alert, interested expressions, you will focus your horrified gaze on that solitary sleeper, so confirming your belief in your inability to speak in public.

The figure opposite illustrates both feedback, which occurs when we reflect on what happened during some activity, and feedforward, the process of anticipation carried out to predict how we are likely to perform.

We can now see how important a role in our lives feedforward and feedback play in determining how well, or poorly, we perform in any given situation. Because we have created a model of the world in our brain, and taught ourselves to perceive that world in a particular way, there is a tendency to notice, and pay attention to anything which appears to confirm our particular outlook on life. When anticipating how we are going to act under a certain set of circumstances we draw on previous experiences to create a theory about our likely performance. Just as a scientist will then test

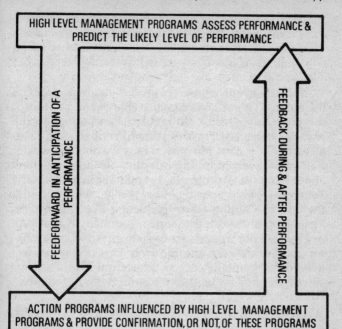

HIGH LEVEL MANAGEMENT PROGRAMS ASSESS PERFORMANCE & PREDICT THE LIKELY LEVEL OF PERFORMANCE

FEEDFORWARD IN ANTICIPATION OF A PERFORMANCE

FEEDBACK DURING & AFTER PERFORMANCE

ACTION PROGRAMS INFLUENCED BY HIGH LEVEL MANAGEMENT PROGRAMS & PROVIDE CONFIRMATION, OR NOT, OF THESE PROGRAMS

out a theory through an experiment, so we seek to validate our theory by behaving in a particular way. If this brings about the expected outcomes then the theory is felt to be sound and we are liable to employ it in future. Where we fail to achieve the anticipated consequences, we may try to modify our theory or explain away the discrepant result in some other way. Only after a long experience of failure will we be prepared to abandon our theory completely.

The stages in the process can be summarised as follows:

* We come to a view about how we are going to behave, ought to behave, will be expected to behave, in some situation.

* We anticipate our level of performance and this influences not only the way we act but also which features of that activity are most likely to be remembered.

After the event we reflect on our conduct, evaluate the amount of success or failure enjoyed and reinforce the programs which both regulated and observed the way we behaved. For this reason feedback and feed-forward are central not only to how we do what we do, but also – even more importantly – to how we think about what we are going to do and have just done. The American psychologist George Kelly, who first put forward the notion of people acting like scientists in setting up and testing theories, commented that: 'All our present perceptions are open to question and recon-sideration . . . even the most obvious occurrences of everyday life might appear utterly transformed if we were inventive enough to construe them differently.'

Analysing Your Own Performance

Prior to carrying out any task of importance to you, analyse your thoughts and actions by asking yourself these two important questions:

1. Which of the ideas in my mind, or the preliminary steps which I am taking to accomplish this activity or task, are positive and constructive?

Focus your attention on these ideas. Make certain that they are realistic. If there are serious difficulties or problems connected with the task you will be undertak-ing, acknowledge these and accept that you are likely to find them hard to overcome. At the same time think about the constructive tactics or strategies which might be used to help you solve them.

A positive feedforward thought might be: 'I know I shall be made anxious by this challenge, but by taking my time and concentrating it should be possible to succeed.'

A negative feedforward idea, when confronting an objectively demanding activity, might be: 'This is going to be easy, I shall cope without any anxiety at all.'

Develop positive thoughts as fully as you can, so as to boost confidence and motivation.

2. Which of the ideas in my mind or the preliminary steps which I am taking to accomplish the task are likely to prove negative and destructive?

Be honest with yourself. Don't hide behind justifications that you know, in your heart, are false. Work to eliminate them either through taking the practical procedures described in later chapters and/or through a reappraisal of your attitudes.

If you have got into a habit of thinking and acting in a particular way this may be tricky at first, but you will be able to bring about changes provided that you are prepared to be as objective as possible about your motives and emotions.

Particularly be on the watch for feelings whose focus is needless fears, self-doubt, apathy, indifference, anger, vengeance or hatred.

In addition to monitoring feedforward I should also like you to carry out feedback analysis. After any activity where you were either critical of or pleased with your performance carry out a short de-briefing session. Note down on a sheet of paper both positive and negative action and management programs. Analyse the cause of each failure to perform as desired, since this will help you to pinpoint the negative programs responsible for the lack of complete success. Similarly, analyse positive outcomes so as to identify those helpful programs which can be used in similar situations in future. Ask yourself:

1. What went right? Note down all the constructive aspects of your performance and how these successes were achieved. In that situation these indicate positive action and management programs.
2. What went wrong? Assess your performance honestly. Ask others for their opinions, so long as you can trust them to provide an objective assessment, but be prepared to rely on your own judgement if this is not possible. Try to work out why things failed to go according to plan. In that situation these indicate negative action and management programs.
3. How can I best improve my performance next time? This is usually the hardest question to answer. Reflect on all you said and did, but avoid becoming too emotionally involved. Be objective. Don't use this as an excuse for punishing yourself.

When carrying out feedback analysis, keep these questions – relating to the presence or absence of four high-level management programs – uppermost in your mind. Unless they are present you will never achieve peak performance or make the most of your mind.

1. Did I honestly believe my action to be appropriate and justified?
2. Was I positive in my actions and attitudes while carrying out that activity?
3. Were my actions and attitudes constructive?
4. Did I use imagination to develop the most effective actions and attitudes?

By exploring your action and management programs in this way you should find it easier to become objective about your strengths and, no less importantly, any weaknesses in the way you approach life's challenges. In Step Three of the training program I shall explain how to develop this skill still further in order to pinpont the precise sources of difficulty and the true causes of failure.

SEVEN

Anxiety in Action

'Anxiety is a wind that blows out the lamp of the mind.'

Arab Proverb

Every program associated with high levels of anxiety has an entirely negative effect on performance. No matter what you are attempting to do, feeling excessively anxious is bound to make you perform less successfully.

Because of anxiety's harmful and pervasive effects, the first step in the Alpha Plan is to learn how these unhelpful responses can be brought under control. In this chapter I want to explain why we become anxious in the first place, since anxiety is usually easier to cope with once its origins and purpose are better understood.

You will also appreciate why neither telling yourself 'not to be silly' nor being told by others to 'pull yourself together' are of any assistance in controlling anxiety or preventing feelings of panic. Indeed, as you may well know from personal experience, the usual effect of such exhortations is to make you even more anxious than before.

Anxiety and Performance

Anxiety harms us both directly and indirectly. Its most obvious and immediate consequences are the familiar symptoms of mental and physical distress: confusion, hesitation, dry mouth, churning stomach, rapidly beating heart and so on. Less obviously, but no less unhelpfully, anxiety causes the brain to run programs designed to reduce these unpleasant feelings. While these may prove very successful, in the short term, their long-term effect is to create significant barriers to self-fulfilment and success.

The optimum level of arousal varies from task to task. For instance, you need to be more relaxed to carry out difficult mental arithmetic than to complete a routine, less intellectually demanding chore. The relationship between arousal and performance follows an inverted U-shaped curve, as shown below.

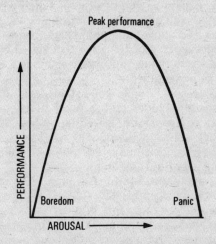

As the diagram shows, increasing arousal enhances our ability to think clearly and act efficiently up to a certain, critical, point. Beyond this limit, however, further increases result in a sharp decline in effectiveness. The key to handling mental and physical arousal successfully, therefore, is to learn how to monitor and regulate these feelings. In this way one can identify the level of arousal at which optimum performance is ensured and then hold it at this point.

Many great actors and actresses, for example, suffer severe stage-fright immediately before the curtain rises. If they allowed those high levels of anxiety to take control, their acting would degenerate into tongue-tied incompetence. By controlling their arousal at the critical level they are able to employ it creatively, transforming nervous energy into magnificent performance.

Negative Coping Strategies

The most widely used anxiety-coping program is avoidance. This may be physical, as when we fake an illness to avoid an unpleasant confrontation at work, or mental as we close our minds to some anxiety-provoking event; 'I don't want to even think about how I did,' says the learner who has made a complete mess of his driving test.

Phobias result from well-established avoidance which usually includes both a physical and a mental refusal to confront the feared stimulus. A spider phobic, for instance, will not only avoid going into any places where spiders may lurk but will often find it distressing even to think about them.

Because avoidance produces such a rapid reduction in uncomfortable feelings it is our most often-employed anxiety-reduction program. But, by denying us the opportunity of practising a skill, acquiring new information or reflecting objectively on our performance, long-term attainment is undermined.

Another popular anxiety reduction program is denial of reality. This is more extreme than avoidance since there is a refusal even to recognise that a problem exists. It's as if the *Titanic*'s captain had tried to reassure passengers by telling them they had just stopped to take on ice! 'My job's safe as houses,' boasts the executive who has denied the reality of his disastrous performance and imminent dismissal. 'We've got a wonderful relationship,' insist the couple whose marriage is on the verge of a total breakdown.

As with avoidance, this program usually has serious long-term consequences since it prevents us from planning for the future and changing to meeting the demands of a rapidly changing world. The Chinese philosopher Lao-Tse sagely remarked, 'The biggest problem in the world could have been solved when it was small.'

Finally, we have a program of 'undoing', the name Freud gave to the strategy of reducing anxiety by resorting to a little 'magic'. Good-luck charms, not walking under ladders, crossing fingers, or avoiding cracks on pavements are all examples of 'undoing', and the more anxiety-arousing any situation is, the more likely it is that people will resort to it.

Unless taken to extremes, at which point it can develop into an obsession, undoing is the least harmful of the negative-coping programs I've described. When used too frequently or believed in too seriously, however, it undermines self-confidence by encouraging people to believe that their destiny lies more with the gods of fortune than in their own hands. This can give rise to a fatalistic attitude and a tendency to be reactive rather than active, to wait on events rather than become master of one's own fate. While the lucky break obviously plays a part in achievement, studies of highly successful men and women, from all walks of life, show that hard work and persistence are far more important than good fortune. As an anonymous writer so aptly put it, 'Success is entirely a matter of luck – ask any failure!'

Whenever you fail to attain an important goal or to perform as well as you had expected, consider if any of these anxiety-reduction programs influenced your approach to that task. Did avoidance, or denial of reality, prevent you from confronting the real issues involved? Have you started depending too much on luck and not enough on your own talents and training?

The Symptoms of Anxiety

When an anxiety-arousing situation is confronted, high levels of physical arousal may disrupt performance by making it extremely hard to think clearly or behave correctly. This is hardly surprising considering anxiety's painful symptoms, which include: rapidly beating heart, fast uneven breathing, increased sweating, a dry mouth, upset stomach, nausea, giddiness, trembling, blushing and cramped muscles. At the same time the mind is usually filled with such negative thoughts as 'I can't cope', 'I'm losing control', 'I'm going to faint', or 'Everyone must be looking at me'. Concentration falters, memory is impaired, routine tasks become harder to perform and more demanding challenges may defeat us entirely.

Anxiety does not always attack both body and mind. Some people become physically tense but remain clearheaded. Others, although their body remains relaxed, become extremely mentally confused. Most often, however, anxiety is an unpleasant mixture of both physical and mental arousal which, when sufficiently intense, may produce a panic attack.

The programs producing these responses are among the most primitive we possess. They have evolved as part of our innate survival mechanism. Unlike avoidance, denial and undoing these are hard-wired into the brain. But while we can never eliminate them we can, fortunately, learn to control them. To see how this is possible we need to look in more detail at the mechanism which produces arousal and see why it evolved in the first place.

The Fight-and-Flight Response

Our early ancestors faced real threats to life and limb as they hunted in the dark forests and open plains. At any moment they might become the prey of a stronger, more ferocious creature; and should that happen, they must either stand and fight or turn and flee. Hence the popular name for the mechanism which evolved to meet this threat, the fight-and-flight response. It is the programs which comprise this response, known technically as the autonomic nervous system (ANS) that trigger the bodily changes associated with rising anxiety. By doing so the ANS both alerts us to danger and motivates us to escape from, or to avoid, harmful and threatening situations.

Let's turn back the clock to prehistoric times and imagine one of our distant forebears out hunting. Suddenly there is noise in the nearby undergrowth. It may be the wind or a small, inoffensive creature; equally it could be a wild and hungry carnivore with a meal in mind. There is no time for deliberation about whether or not the noise spells a genuine danger. If there really is a man-eater in the undergrowth, such a debate would have a fatal outcome. Survival depends on moving almost instantly into a state of high arousal. To fight or to flee efficiently the limbs require increased supplies of food and oxygen. These are carried by the blood, so the heart starts to pump more vigorously. At the same time breathing is increased so as to draw more oxygen into the body and expel carbon dioxide. Blood is diverted away from less essential areas, such as the skin and digestive tract, to make additional supplies available to the arm and leg muscles. The brain, too, needs increased oxygen and glucose in order to think more rapidly.

A human under threat of attack can be likened to a country at war. As soon as the air-raid sirens sound, men and women rush from homes and factories to man the guns and all non-essential, routine work is suspended until the emergency passes. Some parts of your body, such as the digestive system, also 'close down' for the duration of the alert.

For the hunter this almost-immediate response to the prospect of danger might well have meant the difference between life and death. Even today, there are still occasions when we are under physical threat and it is at such times that the fight-and-flight response truly comes into its own.

At such times we may discover remarkable and previously unrealised reserves of stamina, speed and strength as this ancient survival system takes over. The trouble is that these programs are seldom appropriate to the kind of dangers confronting us in the twentieth century, since we are much more likely to face threats to our psychological well-being than our physical safety.

We may feel very anxious, for instance, when faced with somebody who is verbally aggressive, even though there is no risk of our being physically attacked. We will almost certainly be made anxious at the prospect of rejection by someone we love, while attending an interview, sitting an exam, talking with strangers at a party, eating in public, or when faced with any situations, objects, people, places, activities or animals which, for various reasons, have come to be seen as threatening.

In each of these situations the brain responds as if faced with an objective threat to survival. This happens as a result of learning. As infants we possess a general ability to become aroused and, under certain circumstances, to interpret these feelings as anxiety or fear. But we are not born afraid or anxious about anything in particular. You have only to watch a small child toddle cheerfully up to a fierce dog, or wander fearlessly into a busy main road, to realise how little children appreciate the dangers involved.

To safeguard us, parents and other adults teach us to feel fear of certain situations. This may be done through punishment or by warnings: 'Don't cross a busy main road', 'never take sweets from a stranger'.

In the 1920s two psychologists called Watson and Raynor demonstrated how fear could be conditioned in this way by deliberately making an eleven-month-old orphan called Albert phobic about white rats. At first

Albert played happily with the tame rat he was given.
Then, every time they showed him the rat, the
experimenters also made a loud noise which startled
the child. After a short while Albert associated the rat
with the anxiety-arousing noise and transferred his
fears to the animal. Soon even a glimpse of the rat was
sufficient to make him distressed and tearful. You may
be relieved to learn that the psychologists then removed
the phobia, so little Albert did not grow up a rat phobic.
They were able to take away his fears using the same
natural mechanism, which you will learn to control in
the Alpha Plan, the step-down branch of the body's
automatic pilot.

But the point of this experiment was to show that we
can become fearful about virtually anything in the
world through a learning process. In other words the
brain comes to link a particular input, which may be
objectively perfectly harmless, with a subjective threat
to its survival. At this point, without any further debate
or consideration, it switches on the powerful fight-and-
flight response.

Step-Up-Step-Down

Our body has two nervous systems. One controls our
voluntary actions, and we use it whenever we intend to
perform some task, such as opening this book and
turning the pages. The second is the ANS, or fight-and-
flight mechanism, which I have already mentioned. Its
purpose is to take charge of those routine yet vital
bodily activities, such as digesting food, pumping
blood, breathing, and controlling temperature.

The ANS can be likened to the automatic pilot of an
aircraft, flying the body and freeing our minds for other
tasks, such as solving problems, making decisions,
learning, reasoning and enjoying life. Imagine attempting any of those if, seventy times each minute, you had

to order your heart to beat while commanding the lungs to inflate as you supervised body temperature, and instructed your gut to digest your last meal.

There is, however, a price to pay for this automatic control. Because the ANS usually runs its programs independently of those programs concerned with voluntary actions it cannot be obliged to respond to those management programs in the normal course of events.

Returning to the analogy of a multinational company used in earlier chapters, one might compare the ANS to security guards protecting the organisation's key installations. When the alarms sound, these guards, normally responsive to instructions from senior management, assume full control of events. They are empowered, so long as the emergency – or supposed emergency – lasts, to operate entirely according to their own rules for protecting the plants. During this time they disregard all commands and requests from higher authority.

Much the same happens whenever the ANS responds to anything the brain perceives as a threat. Once switched to emergency running your 'thinking brain' cannot countermand that order. Even though you realise that there is no reason for alarm your body continues to respond as if facing an urgent and immediate threat to survival. It doesn't help to tell yourself to calm down and keep cool. Indeed because such instructions have no chance of being obeyed, what usually happens is increased anxiety as you realise that your feelings are out of control.

The changes which have been brought about by the ANS, increased heart rate, rapid breathing, more sweating and so on, can only be corrected and the body returned to normal running by the same mechanism which speeded them up in the first place, that is the autonomic nervous system.

This is possible because the ANS has two branches which, most of the time, work in harmony to create a state of normal arousal. The two branches of the ANS may be compared to the reins of a horse. To keep the animal moving forward in a straight line, the rider applies equal pressure to each side. If more tension is applied to either rein, however, the horse will turn in that direction.

In the ANS these reins consist of two mechanisms. One, which increases arousal, is known technically as the sympathetic branch while the second, which slows the system down again, is called the parasympathetic branch. As you sit watching TV and feeling relaxed and at ease, the slow-down, or parasympathetic, branch is exerting dominance over the system. As a result your heart rate is moderate and breathing slow. When life gets more hectic, however, the speed-up, or sympathetic, branch gains the upper hand, raising heart rate, increasing breathing, sweating and muscular tension. To bring about these bodily changes the ANS relies on chemical messengers, hormones, to carry its instructions to all parts of the body.

The best known of these hormones, adrenalin, has been dubbed 'jungle juice', since it plays such a vital role in the fight-and-flight response. That sharp sensation of discomfort in the pit of your stomach which signals a rise in anxiety is produced by the sudden release of adrenalin.

Imagine that you are strolling across a field, enjoying the scenery and feeling at peace with the world. Suddenly you spot a large bovine creature trotting purposefully towards you and you remember seeing a sign warning that there was a bull about. While your 'thinking' mind is studying the creature and running programs to determine whether the animal is a bull or a docile cow, your inborn, automatic defence programs of the fight-and-flight system go into immediate overdrive as the speed-up branch of the ANS takes command. Adrenalin carries the signals of alarm around in the bloodstream calling the body to action stations. Your heart beats faster, your stomach churns and you experience all the other, familiar, symptoms of fear.

Now suppose that, as the animal gets closer, you realise that it is only a harmless cow. With the danger passed, the slow-down branch of the ANS quickly returns the body to normal running. Your heart stops racing, your breathing becomes regular and shallow again, you no longer sweat. But had it really been a bull that increase in arousal would give you the best chance of escape.

The same arousal occurs, in the absence of any physical danger, whenever there is a threat to your psychological well-being. Suppose you are waiting to be interviewed for an important job. As the minutes tick away and the moment when you must face your interrogation draws closer, doubts creep into your mind. Will you answer their questions successfully or make a fool of yourself and appear a failure?

Your fight-and-flight mechanism interprets these worries in terms of an objective threat to survival and increases the level of arousal. These bodily changes are noted by the 'thinking' areas of the brain which react with further negative thoughts about what lies ahead. You imagine yourself failing miserably and feeling humiliated. These negative management programs increase the strength of the speed-up mechanism and your body becomes still more aroused. Suddenly, you are very anxious indeed, perhaps even in a state of panic – as shown in the anxiety spiral overleaf.

Because you are aware that these fears are foolish, the slow-down branch of the ANS makes attempts to restore the system to normal running. This only makes matters worse, however, since brain and body have now become the battleground for a conflict between the

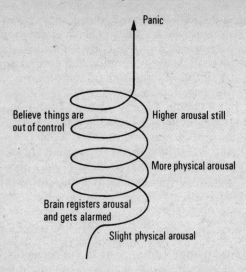

opposing forces of speed-up and slow-down. One is instructing the heart to beat faster and the lungs to work more rapidly, the other attempting to reduce heart rate and ventilation. It is these confusing commands which produce many of the most distressing symptoms of high anxiety. For instance, blood drains from beneath the skin as it is diverted to the muscles with the result that you grow pale. Then it returns causing you to flush. Additional oxygen- and glucose-rich blood reaches the brain. Then the flow is reduced again. As a result you feel lightheaded and giddy. Your muscles tense for action, and then relax again, leaving them feeling like jelly.

All this happens very rapidly since, as I have already explained, the fight-and-flight response is an immediate call to action. It has to work fast, of course, since in a real emergency split seconds might spell the difference between life and death.

We have seen that the ANS, our fight-and-flight

mechanism, can produce arousal extremely swiftly and also that it is not normally under control of management programs. I say not 'normally' because we now know that it is possible, by means of special training techniques, to exert a considerable amount of control over the ANS. Eastern yogis, for example, can survive long periods buried alive in coffins because they are able deliberately to slow down all the major body functions.

This sort of feat requires many years of training and practice to accomplish. But fortunately, one can learn to regulate levels of arousal, so as to achieve the optimum level of each particular activity, fairly quickly and easily.

Mind Control

To see how this mind control can be mastered, we'll consider my earlier comparison between the two branches of the ANS and the reins of a horse. Imagine that the animal has been pulled sharply to the right by an inexperienced rider. In order to return the horse to a straight line the rider must now apply more pressure to the left-hand rein.

Similarly, when the speed-up branch of the ANS has gained the ascendency we can restore the system to normal running by deliberately strengthening the slow-down branch.

This can be done in two main ways. The first is by eating. You may have noticed feeling calmer after a meal. Indeed one reason why some people may have a weight problem is because they munch a chocolate bar or reach for the biscuit barrel whenever they feel anxious. But this is clearly an unsatisfactory solution to everyday anxiety since it only leads to other difficulties as your weight increases and your health declines.

Fortunately there is another way – relaxation. This is the body's natural antidote to anxiety since it is

impossible to be both tense and relaxed at the same
time. Not only does relaxation help you to bring anxiety
under control, but it also permits you to set arousal
levels at any point you wish.

The Relaxation Response

As you will discover when working through Step One
of the Alpha Plan there is nothing especially difficult
about learning to relax. Most people can acquire the
skills needed in just a few weeks of regular practice.
Once mastered these procedures may be used anywhere and at any time to help you cope with stressful or
challenging situations.

Physical relaxation is also the essential starting point
for alpha training since the brain can only be brought
into the right frame of mind for receiving new instructions provided the body is free from needless tension.

PART TWO

The Alpha Plan

'In oneself lies the whole world and if you know how to look and learn, then the door is there and the key is in your hand.'

J. Krishnamurti

As I have already explained, the Alpha Plan is a way of improving all aspects of performance through the enhancement or replacement of negative mental programs. It consists of five steps:

1. Preparing your body. Muscular relaxation produces a stress-free physical environment in which the brain can acquire new programs quickly and easily.
2. Preparing your brain. Training in the production of alpha waves ensures that the brain is highly receptive to these fresh programs.
3. Performance analysis. Before new programs can be created it is essential to analyse the strengths and weaknesses of your current performance carefully and correctly. It then becomes possible to build on any positive features while eliminating the negative aspects of your present approach.
4. Positive mental programming. In this step, the new programs are rehearsed in your imagination prior to tackling them in real life.
5. Peak-performance practice. Programs developed during fantasy training are tried out in real life.

Feedforward and feedback analysis allow you to pinpoint any remaining difficulties and modify the new programs as required to ensure peak performance.

Using the Alpha Plan

Because one can never subtract from the brain's storehouse of knowledge, it is impossible to unlearn any programs. With practice, however, one can develop new and more effective ways of thinking, feeling and acting. Once these programs are well established, the brain uses them in preference to the earlier modes of thought.

As a child, for example, it is likely that you employed a 'counting-up' method for doing simple arithmetic. Given a sum such as 7 plus 5, you probably found the answer by counting upwards from the 7. After a while, however, you memorised the solution to such simple problems so that the answer came immediately to mind. Here the brain has changed from using a slow and unreliable program to one which is faster and more reliable. But you can, of course, always return to a counting-up method should you wish to do so.

Old programs are rather like paths through a dense wood which, having been neglected in favour of other

routes, become overgrown and are very hard to follow. However, sufficient traces of these earlier tracks usually remain for those pathways to be reopened should you wish to do so.

While acquiring a new program do not become discouraged if you sometimes slip into old habits, especially when stressed or anxious. On the learning curve (Chapter Five), such set-backs while mastering any new skill were illustrated as small indentations in the otherwise smoothly rising line. Once the program is firmly established – that is, you have reached the learning curve's plateau – it will be second nature to think, feel and act in this new and more positive manner.

Since short but frequent training sessions are the most effective for mastering any skills, I suggest that you set aside around three weeks at a time when you can practise regularly for about twenty minutes per day; avoid holidays, periods of unusually high activity at work or in the home and so on.

The five steps of the Alpha Plan are given in the sequence they should be learned, with an approximate timetable for each. Because people vary in their ability to master the different skills, regard this as a guide only and don't worry if you find yourself taking more or less time to complete a particular step than I have indicated.

Step One: Preparing Your Body

Introduction

When young we could relax quickly and easily. Sadly, as we grow older we usually grow far more tense. We conceal our emotions by setting the muscles of the face into a mask, and then wonder why we develop tension headaches. We sit or stand in stressful postures and then express surprise when we suffer back pains.

Fortunately it is never too late to regain that childhood ability to relax, unwind and free the muscles from these unnecessary tensions. This skill alone enhances performance and helps to safeguard physical health, by reducing blood pressure and muscular strain, for example. In addition it assists the brain to produce long-duration alpha waves.

It also enables you to adjust your level of arousal to meet the demands of any activity. As I explained in Chapter Seven there are many activities in which one needs to be aroused, in a controlled manner, in order to perform with peak efficiency. When you are tackling some challenging task, such as an examination, or an interview, while making a speech, negotiating a deal, solving a tricky problem, taking a difficult decision, or trying to make an impression on others, a certain level of anxiety sharpens brain and body, allowing positive programs to be run. You feel alert and assured, your reflexes improve and your memory works more efficiently.

By mastering the art of relaxation it becomes possible to establish an optimum level of arousal for each situation you encounter. It also encourages you to confront anxiety-arousing situations through an increase in self-confidence over your ability to use these feelings creatively.

I am going to teach you four different ways of relaxing, each appropriate to a particular circumstance.

The first, basic relaxation, is the foundation on which you construct your other skills. Each session lasts approximately twenty minutes and you should try to set aside this amount of time each day for at least three weeks. After this the skills can be maintained at a high level of proficiency by practising just once or twice each week. Many find it the ideal way of drifting off into a deep, truly restful sleep.

The second skill, rapid relaxation, may be used on any occasion when you feel the need to unwind rapidly. It takes less than fifteen seconds to complete, yet eases away tensions very efficiently. This form of relaxation is useful immediately prior to undertaking some stressful activity, as a means of reviving mind and body after a long journey, or at any time during the day that you feel yourself becoming tense and irritable.

Invisible relaxation helps release tensions so unobtrusively that it can be used in virtually any situation no matter how public.

Finally there is active relaxation, a skill which enables you to remain free from mental and physical stresses while carrying out everyday activities in both work and play.

But first, let me warn you in advance of two frequently encountered difficulties when learning both relaxation and alpha production.

As they feel themselves starting to unwind some

people immediately tense up again. This is because needless muscular tension has become such a habit that being freed from inner stress seems somehow unnatural. Some years ago the New York transit authorities closed down an overhead railway in one part of the city. Shortly afterwards the police began to receive phone calls from people living alongside the abandoned track complaining of strange noises in the night, yet investigations showed no grounds for these complaints. What had happened was that the residents had grown so used to the clatter of trains that the silence seemed strange and caused them to conjure noises out of their imaginations. It's much the same when you start relaxing. The absence of familiar tensions seems strange and even slightly scary. So don't worry if early training sessions involve this see-sawing between tension and relaxation. It is perfectly normal and will disappear once you become more skilled in the procedures.

A second common problem is that of intrusive thoughts. Just when you are starting to feel at peace, a disturbing or distracting idea drifts into your mind. If this happens, neither dwell on the thought nor fight it. Simply notice what has happened and then return your attention to the feelings of relaxation. You should then find that the distracting idea quickly vanishes.

Preparing for Basic Relaxation

You can carry out the basic relaxation training at any time of the day, although I suggest the evening – immediately prior to bed – as being the most appropriate time. The chief difficulty about this is that you may fall asleep before the session ends. If this happens frequently then change to the morning or early afternoon, although you may still like to carry out the procedures last thing at night in order to enjoy more restful sleep.

Set aside twenty minutes during which you are unlikely to be interrupted. Choose a quiet room, take the phone off the hook, and sit or lie down. It doesn't matter which position you adopt so long as you feel comfortable. Some people prefer to stretch out on their bed, or a couch, others to lie on the floor, or sit in an armchair. You may wish to draw the curtains or dim the lights. Again it is a matter of personal preference and I suggest that you experiment so as to find surroundings where you feel most at ease. Loosen tight clothing and take off your shoes. Uncross your legs and rest your arms by your sides.

After reading through the basic relaxation instructions a few times, and studying the illustrations, you should find it quite easy to remember the sequence of movements needed. Alternatively you may prefer to record them on a cassette and then follow those taped instructions, at least for the first few sessions. (I have recorded a cassette based on this part of the book, details of which can be found in the Appendix.)

You will be alternately tensing and relaxing all the major muscle groups in turn in order to become aware of needless tensions and eliminate them. To remember each stage of the procedure use this memory-jogger:

A Soothing Feeling – Totally At Peace

The first letter of each word identifies one of the six stages in relaxing body and brain:

A = Arms and hands
S = Shoulders and neck
F = Face (forehead, jaw, tongue, eyebrows)
T = Torso (chest and stomach)
A = Ankles, legs and buttocks

P = Pictures which help soothe the mind and prepare it for the alpha training taught in Step Two

Timetable: Week One

During this period I suggest that you concentrate
entirely on mastering this basic relaxation. Proceed to
the next procedure only when you are able to release
tensions in the major muscle groups. Continue practising regularly for two or three weeks at least and
then sustain the skill with at least one and preferably
more sessions each week.

Instructions for Basic Relaxation

While lying or sitting down carry out the following
movements.

Close your eyes lightly, rest your head against the
chair or bed, flop out your arms and let your legs go
limp. Keep your breathing light and steady, without
pausing between each breath.

Each time you breathe out repeat the word *calm*
silently to yourself and, as you do so, imagine all your
tensions and worries flowing from your body with
every exhaled breath.

Spend a few moments practising this light, uninterrupted, breathing and repeating *calm* to yourself each
time you breathe out. Now start on the first group of
muscles:

Arms and Hands

Tense the muscles of your fingers, wrists and fore-
arms as follows. Make fists, clenching your hands as
tightly as possible. At the same time attempt to touch
the back of your wrists to your collar bone. Hold this

tension for a slow count to five. Now let go, rest your hands beside you and allow them to relax as completely as you can.

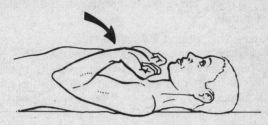

While tensing each group of muscles, during this exercise, notice whether any other muscles also tighten up. For instance when clenching your fists, see whether your jaw or forehead also get more tense. It often happens that we have learned to put unrelated muscles under tension simultaneously, a response which often makes it far harder to perform efficiently. In the example above, an anxious clenching of the fists while giving a talk might cause speaking difficulties or produce a distressing tension headache. If you do become aware of such related tensions, pay special attention to these triggers, since by eliminating needless stress here, you will automatically reduce tension elsewhere in the body.

As you lie still and quiet, your hands limp and relaxed, imagine the stress flowing out of the fingers and vanishing away into the room. Spend a few moments focusing on your breathing, which should remain light and even. Repeat the word *calm* silently as you breathe out and feel the tension seeping away from your hands, arms and shoulders.

Shoulders and Neck

As there is usually a great deal of needless tension in these muscles, the different groups should be treated one at a time.

Press your head against the bed or chair to tense the neck muscles. Hold for a slow count to five. Relax and let your head rest back lightly. As before, keep your breathing regular and light, silently saying the word *calm* with each expelled breath and, as you exhale, picture the neck muscles becoming more and more deeply relaxed.

Next, tense the muscles in your shoulders by hunching them as hard as you can. Lift them upwards. Hold this tension, as before, for a slow count to five. Drop your shoulders and relax them. Feel the tension flowing away from your neck and shoulders; deepen this sensation by focusing on the word *calm* and imagining all your stress being expelled from these muscles with each exhaled breath.

Face

Tense the muscles of jaw and tongue by clenching the teeth and pressing the tongue against the roof of your mouth. Maintain this tension for a slow count to five.

Let go, part the jaws slightly and allow the tongue to rest loosely in your mouth. As before, feel the tension seeping out of the jaw and tongue, down the arms and

 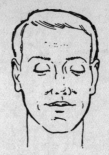

out via the finger tips. Each time you repeat the word *calm* imagine a little more stress being gently soothed from your body.

To tense the muscles of the forehead and around the eyes, close your eyes tightly, pressing the lids firmly together. As you do so screw up your forehead in a frown. Hold this tension for the slow count to five and then let go.

Allow the lids to rest lightly together and unwrinkle the brow. Imagine all the tension seeping away, flowing down the arms and leaving your body via the fingertips.

Concentrate on your breathing and silently repeat the word *calm* each time you breathe out.

Torso

These muscles are easily tensed. Take a deep breath, inhale as hard as you can until the chest cannot expand any further. At the same time flatten your stomach as though anticipating a blow. Hold both your breath and stomach tension for the same slow count to five.

Exhale completely and loosen your stomach muscles as you do so. Allow all these muscles to flop right out. Feel the tension draining away from the body and leaving you very calm and relaxed.

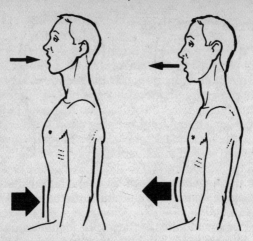

Ankles, Legs and Buttocks

Place these under tension by stretching your legs, pointing your toes, and squeezing your buttocks tightly together. Stretch, point and squeeze.

Hold this for a slow count to five and then let your legs relax again. Feel the tension streaming out through your toes and vanishing into the room, leaving you feeling extremely calm and relaxed. Notice the absence of tension throughout all these major muscle groups. Continue breathing quietly and lightly and repeat the word *calm* on every exhaled breath. As you say this silently to yourself imagine the sense of calm filling your whole being.

Pictures in the Mind

When you have relaxed your body, quieten your mind by picturing yourself transported to some peaceful, sunny seashore. You are warm and secure. You have no fears or tensions. All around you is beauty. Blue skies, the sun shining down, soft sand to lie on and a calm, peaceful sea gently lapping the golden beach. This is your own special place where you can return any time you start to feel stressed, tense or anxious.

Imagine that lovely scene as vividly as you can. Feel the warm sand under your body. Smell the sweet scent of tropical flowers. Hear the soft rustle of palm fronds. Notice the gentle breeze on your hair. Listen to the sea as small waves break against the beach and then retreat. Taste a cooling fruit juice. You feel very relaxed and at peace. You are very safe. There is no tension, no anxiety to disturb your mind.

Spend the next few minutes resting quietly and holding that beautiful scene in your mind. Breathe lightly and silently repeat the word *calm* with each exhalation. Imagine that, as the waves retreat from the beach they carry away with them the last of your fears and worries. You now feel very relaxed and at peace with yourself.

There is no tension in your muscles and your mind is at ease. Focus on these feelings and enjoy them. You are at peace with yourself. Free from stress. Free from tension. Free from anxiety. You are warm, contented, and secure.

Now, place the first two fingers of each hand on your forehead, about mid-way between your eyebrows and the hairline. Your fingertips should easily locate two small areas of raised bone beneath the skin.

When you have identified them apply a light pressure with your fingertips and, while doing so, repeat to yourself: 'At any time and in any situation I need only

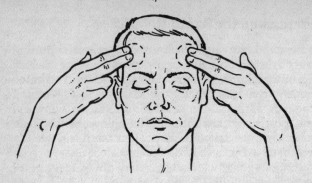

do this for my anxieties to diminish leaving me feeling relaxed and confident.'

Massage the skin gently with your fingertips for a moment or two and repeat that instruction over a number of times. Now rest your hands back at your sides and spend a while enjoying the feelings of being deeply relaxed.

Count slowly backwards from 5 to 1 and when you reach 1, open your eyes and rise unhurriedly from the chair or bed. Do not stand up quickly or you may feel slightly giddy.

Go about your next task calmly and try to carry these feelings of relaxation into your normal routine. Continue to practice basic relaxation until you are able to unwind your muscles without too much difficulty and can create and hold on to that pleasant, soothing, image without too much difficulty or distraction.

Timetable: Week Two

I suggest that you start learning rapid relaxation around Day 8 of your training programme. Continue with the basic relaxation while doing so.

Instructions for Rapid Relaxation

Find a quiet, private, place where you can sit down, loosen tight clothing and remove your shoes.

Sit still for a few moments, eyes closed and with the lids resting lightly together. Focus on your breathing which, as with basic relaxation, should be light and even, flowing in and out without any pause between inhalation and exhalation. Repeat the word *calm* silently to yourself with each outward breath. Massage your forehead as instructed above and allow feelings of peace and tranquillity to fill your mind.

Now place all the muscles under tension at the same time by carrying out each of the stressing techniques you have learned during basic relaxation training:

Clench your fists.
Try and touch wrists to shoulders.
Hunch your shoulders.
Frown and screw up your eyes.
Clench your teeth and push your tongue against the roof of the mouth.
If there is a support behind your head, press back firmly.
Stretch your legs, squeeze your buttocks together and point your toes.
Take a deep breath and flatten your stomach as though about to receive a blow.

Place your body under tension in this way for a slow count to four. Now, stretch your fingers. Roll your shoulders. Unclench your jaw and let the mouth sag open slightly, open your eyes and smooth out the forehead. Wriggle your toes and bend your legs. Move your tongue around in your mouth.

Finally allow these muscles to flop out and relax completely. Close your eyes lightly together and, as before, place the first and second fingers of each hand on the forehead relaxation points.

Bring to mind that picture of that peaceful beach and breathe slowly, repeating the word *calm* with every exhalation.

Massage the pressure points very lightly with your fingertips and feel all the tensions, anxieties and worries flowing from your mind and body. Do this for 10 or 15 seconds, then open your eyes slowly and, just as slowly, stand up and go about your affairs.

Rapid relaxation may be carried out easily and conveniently several times each day. It will allow you to control needless physical arousal under almost any circumstances and helps to ensure that unhelpful bodily reponses are not going to trigger negative mental programs.

Timetable: Week Two

Invisible relaxation can be started at the same time as rapid relaxation.

Instructions for Invisible Relaxation

Because there is no need to tense the muscle groups you can make use of this procedure while attending a meeting, travelling on public transport, at a social gathering or in any situation where it is difficult, or impossible, to enjoy the privacy needed to put into practice the other forms of relaxation I have described.

Start by spending a few moments noticing your breathing so that it becomes slow and light without any pause between the inhalations and exhalations. Keep the air flowing smoothly and evenly in and out of your lungs. Each time you breathe out, repeat the word *calm* and imagine your tensions being expelled from the mind with every exhalation.

Now focus your attention on your dominant hand: the right if you are right-handed, the left if left-handed. You are going to train yourself to raise the temperature in one hand. By doing so you can induce a state of relaxation.

There are a number of techniques for hand-warming and I suggest that you experiment with the three I am about to describe to discover which works best for you.

The first method is to concentrate on the selected hand and imagine that you can feel heat rising from the palm and fingers. With a little practice you should start to gain a distinct impression of increased warmth.

The second is to picture yourself holding your hand before a cosy fire.

Thirdly, you can hold the chosen hand a short distance away from your cheek, which is a hot spot, and feel heat flowing from the face and heating up the palm.

The sensation of increased heat is no illusion. Using a suitable thermometer it is perfectly possible to monitor these changes. Why does the hand get hotter? Simply because, as I explained in Chapter Seven, relaxation causes an increase in blood-flow to vessels directly beneath the skin. By directing more blood to just one hand, therefore, you both raise its temperature and become more relaxed by strengthening the slow-down branch of the body's fight-and-flight mechanism.

Timetable: Week Three

Start using active relaxation from around Day 14 onwards. By this time you should have become far more aware, than before, of needless muscle tensions.

Instructions for Active Relaxation

This involves permitting any muscles which do not have to be kept tense to remain as relaxed as possible.

By doing so you keep your overall levels of arousal comfortably low and protect yourself against stress.

At the end of a basic relaxation session, stand up slowly and then, instead of going about your everyday chores right away, spend a little longer focusing on each of the body's main muscle groups in turn as you move slowly about the room.

Start by paying attention to the muscles in your hands, wrists and arms. Are they tense? Have you clenched the fingers into a fist or are they hanging loosely at your side? Are your arms under unnecessary tension or have they remained comfortably relaxed?

Notice whether your shoulders have become tense again. If so ease away this tension with a few small, circular movements before letting drop down and relax.

Test each of the muscle groups in this way, looking out for needless tension and relaxing it away. Concentrate on letting the muscles unwind more and more completely.

Is your spine held straight? It performs most efficiently when vertical and is least vulnerable to damage. Are your shoulders hunched? Are you frowning or furrowing your brow? Pay attention to the ways in which you are making your body work. Be aware of its needs and alert to its problems.

With practice you will become sensitive to this unhelpful tension and relax automatically. At first, however, you will need to direct your attention to all the major muscle groups in turn and actively unwind them.

As you perform everyday activities, take some time, every so often, to search out these unhelpful tensions. Special danger zones are muscles of the shoulders, neck and face.

If you are sitting at a desk, or behind the driving wheel, for long periods, make sure you carry out this muscle check regularly, since it is very easy to stress muscles badly through poor posture.

Summary of Step One

The first step in Alpha-Plan training is to learn relaxation. Four procedures for regaining control over the physical tension should be mastered.

Basic relaxation – the skill to be acquired first since it provides the foundation on which to build the other, more rapid, procedures. Basic relaxation helps to reduce stress and improves both mental and physical health by increasing your tolerance for daily challenges.

Rapid relaxation – for use immediately prior to some anxiety-arousing activity, and as a technique for reducing general levels of stress.

Invisible relaxation – based on a simple hand-warming procedure which can be used in a wide range of situations, either as an anxiety-stopper or in order to program more positive thoughts and attitudes into the mind.

Active relaxation – may be used while performing everyday activities. It reduces the overall level of bodily tension and so enables you to perform physical tasks more efficiently while, at the same time, safeguarding you against any sudden rises in stress.

Most people require around three weeks of practice to develop a reasonable proficiency in relaxation. But, as I have already explained, you should not feel concerned if it takes you somewhat longer than this. The essential thing is not speed but mastery. Continue to practise and use all four relaxation procedures while working on the remaining steps in this program. After two weeks of this training you should be ready to proceed to the second step of the Plan.

Step Two: Preparing Your Brain

Introduction

Positive mental programing demands a relaxed body and a receptive frame of mind. The diagram below, adapted from one devised by Maxwell C. Cade, shows how changes in physical arousal (indicated by the vertical line) and brain waves (the horizontal line) combine to produce four states.

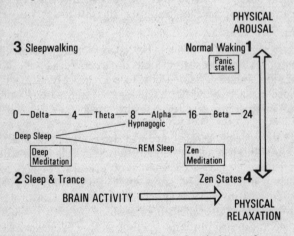

The fourth state, where low levels of physical arousal are combined with slow-frequency brain waves, mainly alpha but with some low beta and high theta, produces the relaxed alertness at which the mind is most receptive to new programs. When this is achieved the brain becomes mindful in the Buddhist sense of having an aware attentiveness without distractions. It is this state of mind you will learn to enter in Step Two of the Alpha Plan.

Although brain-wave research employs all the complex electronic paraphernalia of the modern laboratory, the procedures used for producing this fourth state of consciousness are often derived from the most ancient Eastern meditative practices.

The procedure used in this step of the program, Zazen, (the word means 'sitting with Zen') is both easy to master and very effective in creating the conditions of the fourth state.

EEG recordings have shown that Zazen is accompanied by low alpha brain waves (around 8 Hz) combined with steady theta at about 4.5 Hz and a significant decrease in physical arousal associated with deep relaxation. Studies of Japanese Zen masters during Zazen indicated that, in less than one minute, the fast beta waves associated with problem-solving gave way to fast alpha at between 11 and 12 Hz, with amplitudes ranging from 45 to 50 microvolts. Thirty minutes later low-frequency alpha together with some theta appeared, these patterns of waves lasting several minutes after meditation ceased.

Akira Kasamatsu and Tomio Hirai of Tokyo University have divided Zen meditation into four stages:

1. The appearance of alpha with open eyes (harder than with closed eyes).
2. Increase in alpha amplitude (i.e. higher voltages).
3. Decrease in alpha frequency (further slowing of brain waves).
4. The production of a 'rhythmical theta train.'

During his work as a consultant to the Menninger

Foundation, Swami Rama provided demonstrations of the brain's ability to control a wide variety of brain waves and bodily functions. Researchers reported that he was able to produce 70 per cent alpha waves over a five-minute period by thinking of an empty blue sky with a 'small white cloud' sometimes going by. He commented after several sessions that 'alpha isn't anything. It is literally nothing.'

Krishnamurti, the Indian philosopher, said:

> In its beginning, meditation is an exercise of attention . . . Attention has no border, no frontier to cross; attention is clarity, clear of all thought. Thought is the cessation of meditation; good meditation begins with the cessation of thought. Awareness of this is to be attentive . . . Meditation is not an intellectual process, which is still within the area of thought. Meditation is the freedom from thought . . .

Alpha Training

In the thousands of years during which meditation has been explored and expanded, many different methods for producing the desired mental state have been developed. Some use mental images, others an external object such as a candle, a lamp, or a mandala (religious symbol), yet others stress the need for a total withdrawal from the senses. Some demand inactivity; a few vigorous physical exercise, as in the whirling dances of the Dervishes.

The experience of alpha – that is, when the brain is producing alpha waves – varies from person to person. For most it is a pleasant, relaxed and enjoyable feeling, although some people report no change in their feelings, even though the EEG is clearly recording alpha wave-patterns. A minority, however, may be distressed by this state of mind at first, because having spent so much of their adult life in frenetic mental activity and being far more used to the effects of beta than alpha, the tranquillity of alpha, paradoxically, arouses a slight amount of anxiety and apprehension. But even if you experience these difficulties at first, do persevere because the benefits are considerable.

Research has shown that meditation, on its own, helps reduce anxiety, enhance learning, bring about better physical and mental health and increase resistance to stress-related fatigue.

By following the procedures described below, however, you should find it possible to acquire these important new skills without too much difficulty. If, at any time during your training sessions, you start to feel mentally or physically uncomfortable simply stop at that point and return to the procedure later that day or the following day. Never proceed unless you feel entirely comfortable and at ease with yourself.

Preparing for Alpha Training

Several factors may influence your ability to develop an alpha state:

1. Diet

Prepare for each session by avoiding alcohol, cigarettes, tea or coffee and any other stimulants or sedatives for at least an hour prior to practice. What you eat, as well as how much, may also be a factor to take into account. Recently a number of researchers have drawn attention to the role of diet on mood. In one study Dr John Crayton, associate professor of psychiatry at the University of Chicago Medical Center, found a significant link between eating wheat or drinking milk and depression, irritability, fatigue and confused thinking.

At Texas Tech. University in Lubbock, Dr Bonnie

Spring and her colleagues have discovered an associa-
tion between drowsiness, leading to inferior performance, and the type of low-protein, high-carbohydrate
meals with which millions of Europeans and Americans
start their day. The message from their research is that
one should eat protein (meat, fish, cheese) to remain
alert and carbohydrate-rich meals (bread, waffles,
cakes) in order to sleep more easily. This is because
carbohydrates eaten alone increase the brain's uptake
of the amino acid tryptothan and this, in turn, stimu-
lates the production of a neurotransmitter called
serotonin which has a sedating effect.

Because there are such substantial individual differences in our reaction to foods the only way to find out
whether your diet is helpful or harmful to alpha production is to monitor training sessions; for a sample
record form see Fig. 3.

2. Surroundings

For the early sessions you will probably find it easier to
practise in a quiet, perhaps slightly darkened room
which is sufficiently warm for you to remain inactive for
approximately twenty minutes without feeling either
too hot or too cold. With experience it is possible to
achieve the desired state of mind under far less favour-
able conditions.

You may also discover that different colour schemes
have an effect on your response to training. Blues and
greens, for instance, are able to soothe both mind and
body. Merely being in a room decorated with either of
these colours has been found to lower blood pressure,
reduce heart-rate and slow respiration.

Red, by comparison, acts directly on the speed-up
(sympathetic) branch of the autonomic nervous system
to produce increased arousal, and should obviously be
avoided.

Dark browns and other rather drab colours make

some people feel depressed during alpha training, but colour preference is clearly a very personal matter and I suggest that you experiment, so far as your surroundings allow, with different schemes.

3. *Posture and Position*

Some people find it easiest to brain-train while seated cross-legged on the floor with their spine kept vertical. Certainly if you are sitting down it is important to hold your body correctly so that none of the muscles are sending tension signals to the brain and the abdomen is not uncomfortably compressed. This does not mean adopting a 'drill square' posture, but rather placing yourself in a position where all the muscle groups feel at their most relaxed and stress-free. If sitting in a chair make certain the lower back is fully supported, if necessary by placing a small cushion between the back of the seat and the lumbar region.

Finally, you may find it interesting to try facing different directions during early training sessions, to see whether moving around the points of the compass enhances or diminishes your power of concentration.

4. *Time of day*

Practising at different times of the day can also prove useful since the body's natural rhythms exert a potent influence over both emotions and level of alertness. Gay Gaer Luce, author of *Body Time*, says:

> Most people don't realise how much they change over twenty-four hours. They may notice that they get particularly tired at 2 a.m., or chilly late in the evening . . . [However] they remain largely unaware of changing immunity to infection or stress (which drops at night) or the fact that blood pressure, mood, pulse, respiration, blood-sugar

levels . . . and our ability to handle drugs all rise
and fall in a circadian rhythm.

Body temperature rises by around half a degree
during the first three hours after waking, a time associated with the most consistent improvements in efficiency. In a study conducted by Dr Karl Klein at the
Institute for Flight Medicine in Bad Godesberg, Ger-
many, the mental performance of volunteers was found
to peak from 1 o'clock in the afternoon to 7 o'clock in the
evening. During this period physical fitness was
greatest, and they produced the best results on tests of
reaction times and motor-co-ordination. The worst
results, on all aspects of mental and physical performance measured, were obtained between 2 and 6 o'clock
in the morning, even for people who normally work at
that time.

Similarly the brain's spontaneous production of
alpha varies around the clock. Continuous EEG recordings have shown that both the frequency and amplitude
of these waves can vary from one hour to the next.

I suggest that you start by choosing any convenient
time to practise, but be prepared to change your
schedule if unexpected difficulties are encountered.

5. Using Music

French researcher Mme Belanger considers that listening to Mozart 'co-ordinates breathing, cardio-vascular
rhythm and brain-wave rhythm and leads to positive
effects on health. It acts on the unconscious, stimulating receptivity and perception.' Steve Halpern, an
American music therapist, talks of 'sound nutrition',
explaining that 'Music is not just a metaphor that we
hear a while and then leave. You actually "hear" the
music when you are playing it back in your own
nervous system . . . So it is that music nourishes the
body.' Music, he says, massages the body's organs,

changes hormone levels, reduces stress, and increases the capacity for learning.

But not all music is beneficial. In one investigation, volunteers were asked to extend their right arm horizontally and then to resist as strongly as they could when the experimenters attempted to push their arm down. After a period of relaxation their resistance was tested again under one of two conditions, listening either to rock (Led Zeppelin) or to classical music. When rock was played the resistance of every subject was weakened, while listening to classical music was found to have either a neutral or a strengthening effect.

In this book *The Dance of Life*, anthropologist Edward Hall comments that response to familiar, middle-range frequency rhythms, such as those found in music and dance, are a universal phenomenon. All over the world people can be seen 'syncing when music is played.' But there is, claims Hall, a widespread misconception about music:

Because there is a beat to music, the generally accepted belief is that the rhythm originates in the music, not that *music is a highly specialised releaser of rhythms already in the individual*. Otherwise how does one explain the close fit between ethnicity and music? Music can also be viewed as a rather remarkable extension of the rhythms generated in human beings.

Soothing music can greatly enhance alpha training. Of particular value is Baroque music: that composed during the half century from 1700 onwards and including such composers as Handel, Bach, Telemann, Corelli and Vivaldi. The latter, incidentally is also known to have a wonderfully calming effect on infants and will often send a fretful baby to sleep.

A possible explanation for Baroque music's special

ability to induce a sense of calm, relaxed, well-being is to be found in its structural characteristics. The aim of eighteenth-century composers was symmetry throughout their music. Early in the composition they clearly established their main key, the first and final movements were in the tonic key and the slow movement in a closely related key. Baroque composers sought to create an ideal mathematical form and harmony in their music, to produce a unity that would help free the mind from wordly worries. They also introduced contrasts, between movements and between instruments, between the treble melody and the bass accompaniment. The overall result was that contrast created a harmonious unit.

Mendelssohn once remarked: 'Music cannot be expressed in words, not because it is vague but because it is more precise than words.'

In their desire to achieve mathematically perfect harmony, the Baroque composers succeeded in writing music whose frequency is precisely tuned to generate the beta/alpha/theta brain-wave mixture whose subjective state is relaxed awareness.

I suggest, therefore, that you experiment with different types of classical music from this period to see whether any particular composition enhances your training sessions. Listening on earphones offers the additional benefit of shutting out any loud and unexpected sounds from outside – a door slamming, car backfiring and so on – which would easily break your concentration.

6. Record-keeping

During training it is helpful to have a record of each session. I have provided a sample form for this purpose, which should be copied into a suitable notebook and completed immediately following practice (Fig. 3).

By examining your notes you should be able to identify the conditions best suited to your training needs.

Fig. 3 Brain-training Record Form

Session number:

Day:

Date:

Time of day of training session:

Surroundings: (*Include any details you feel may have influenced your feelings, such as the room – its size, too warm or too cold, noisy or quiet, darkened or well lit, colour scheme and so on.*)

Food and drink taken prior to session: (*Write down anything you ate or drank within two hours of starting to practice.*)

Music played:

Posture: (*Sitting or lying, eyes open or closed, which direction were you facing – i.e. north, south, east or west.*)

Mood: (*Note whether you felt happy or sad, tired or energetic, angry or relaxed.*)

Success of session: (*Did you find it easy to focus on your breathing and to prevent your mind from wandering? Were you distracted by everyday worries or did you start feeling anxious soon after your felt yourself growing more relaxed? I suggest you rate each session on a scale of 7 to 0. If you felt calm, relaxed and were able to focus clearly on your breathing then you might rate the session at 6 or 7. If you found yourself easily distracted and unable to continue for long without growing more tense and anxious instead of more relaxed and calm, then the session should be rated at 0 or 1.*)

Timetable: Week Three

You should start alpha training after spending around two weeks on Step One. Being able to relax physically will greatly assist you in entering the fourth state and producing the mixed alpha waves required.

Instructions for Alpha Training

Start by carrying out a session of physical relaxation. Choose any of the three methods suggested in Step One of the training which involve relaxing while either seated or lying. At first you may prefer to use either the basic procedure, if you have enough time, or rapid relaxation. As you become more experienced and confident of your ability to banish bodily tensions successfully, the hand-warming procedure should prove sufficient.

Still sitting or lying in the comfortable position spend a few more minutes retreating to that peaceful, secure and comfortable scene which you created at the end of the basic training session.

Now sit upright and, with your eyes remaining lightly closed, begin to focus on your breathing. Breath in a slow, relaxed way without pausing between breaths, so that the air passes in and out of your lungs in an uninterrupted flow.

Focus all your attention on breathing. At first this may be slightly difficult with unwanted thoughts distracting you and undermining your concentration. If this happens, simply return your attention to the rhythm of your breathing.

Intensify this concentration by using a Zazen procedure. This involves counting your breaths, silently to yourself, from 1 to 10 and then starting all over again.

As you do so imagine a coin being dropped into a deep well which opens at a point close to the top of your skull and extends through your body to the ground beneath.

Release the coin as you begin breathing out. As the breath flows effortlessly from your lungs, picture that coin drifting slowly and gently down through the well water so that it reaches the bottom as the last bit of air is expelled from your lungs. Each coin drops on to the one before it, producing a pile of ten coins, at which point you start the process all over again.

By focusing on your breathing and using the image of the coin to help reduce distracting thoughts from entering the mind, you should find it relatively easy to train your mind to produce the necessary state of relaxed awareness. If electrodes were attached to your scalp and the brain signals fed to an EEG, it would indicate sustained alpha production combined with some beta at the upper end and theta at the lower end of the frequency.

Keep the training sessions fairly short at first and build up slowly until you are able to meditate for 10 or 15 minutes without difficulty or becoming too distracted. There is, of course, no reason why you should not meditate for much longer if you find it agreeable and relaxing to do so. However, fifteen minutes is quite long enough as far as the Alpha Plan is concerned.

Immediately before the end of the session, place the first and second finger of each hand against the sides of your temple and say to yourself: 'At any time I can create this state of mind merely by doing this . . .'

By repeating this action a number of times you should find it increasingly easy to return mind and body to the desired state of relaxed alertness merely by employing this trigger.

After each session get up *slowly*. This is important after any exercises involving relaxation or breathing because you may well feel slightly giddy. This effect is simply due to temporary changes in the blood supply reaching the brain and is nothing to feel concerned about as it quickly disappears.

Continue with these regular practice sessions for another fourteen days. After this you should have at least four sessions per week, whether or not you wish to bring about changes in mind programs. As with any other skill, alpha training needs to be practised in order to sustain a high level of performance.

Once you are confident of your ability to focus on your breathing and to remain mentally and physically relaxed for up to fifteen minutes you are ready to move on to Step Four of the Alpha Plan and start reprogramming your brain.

In order to do so, however, you must first have a very clear idea of exactly what it is about your present ways of thinking, feeling and behaving in a particular situation you wish to change. This requires a careful performance analysis, using procedures described in Step Three of the training program.

You can start on this part of the training right away so that by the time body and brain have been trained to enter the fourth state on command you will be all ready to provide yourself with effective new programs.

Step Three: Performance Analysis

Before you start trying to correct mistakes in performance it is essential to identify the reasons for those failures clearly and precisely. As computer pioneers Marvin Minsky and Seymour Papert have commented, 'learning to learn is very much like debugging complex computer programs. To be good at it requires one to know a lot about describing processes and manipulating such descriptions.'

Discovering what's going wrong with action programs is often fairly straightforward. A tennis player may realise, for example, that her backhand is letting her down; the learner driver that poor clutch control makes him stall on hills; the maths' student that carelessness in checking answers is responsible for foolish mistakes in his calculations. Indeed, a primary task of coaches, instructors and teachers is to provide both the practical advice necessary to bring about such improvements in performance and also objective feedback about the students' performance. However, as we have seen, action programs can often only be significantly improved upon once negative management programs have been identified and corrected.

In this step of the program I am going to describe two ways of analysing your performance in order to diagnose, as precisely as possible, the reasons for any failures in performance.

The first method, which I call differencing, helps identify both the positive and negative aspects of any performance. Fourteen questions enable you to clarify in your mind both what is going wrong *and* what is going right in any activity. This is important since, as I explained in Part One, almost every performance contains both successes and failures, both things you do well and those you do poorly. Adopting too global a view of any outcome means that one tends to pay insufficient attention to either the good or bad features of that attempt. If you concentrate solely on errors then your feedback will prove excessively negative, which is likely to decrease motivation while increasing anxiety. On the other hand, focusing solely on your attainments can result in an overly rigid attitude which prevents you from adapting performance to meet changing conditions.

The second method of analysis I describe, mind-mapping, allows you to create a two-dimensional chart of your performance on any task. By comparing activities in which you succeed with those where you usually fail, you can arrive at a more accurate understanding of the relative importance of action and management programs.

Differencing

Select some activity which is important to you and where your performance leaves you feeling dissatisfied. Ideally choose one which you will attempt on a number of occasions over the next couple of weeks. If this is not possible, then you will have to depend on your memory of past attempts to provide some, or all, of the answers.

While carrying out the analysis, make no attempt to change your behaviour, even if you realise how it might be improved upon. If you do alter your approach or attitude during the course of analysis, the results will be very hard to interpret.

Include the widest possible range of circumstances in

which you have carried out that task. If the focus of your analysis was playing a sport, for example, you should consider your performance when playing both friendly and competitive games, when opposed by friends as well as strangers, while being partnered by people you know and those with whom you have not previously played, when being watched by a few members of your family or under the scrutiny of a large audience.

If you were concerned to improve public speaking, then as well as formal talks to a large group, you should include off-the-cuff, after-dinner speeches, presentations to colleagues, subordinates, superiors and so on. The more situations considered, the more informative and helpful the analysis is likely to prove.

Use the two case histories provided as a guide to the type of information which each question seeks to extract in order to pinpoint the reasons behind faulty performance.

Performance Analysis
While attempting this activity: What do I usually do wrong? What do I usually do right? What is distinctive about my failure? Where do I usually do it wrong? Where do I usually do it right? What's different about the places where I do it wrong? When do I usually do it wrong? When do I usually do it right? What's different about the circumstances when I do it right? With whom or what is my failure usually associated? With whom or what is my failure not usually associated? How often do I fail? How often do I succeed? What is different about these two situations?

The first sample analysis was prepared by Carol, a 36-year-old office manager, who described her problem as follows:

> I am hopeless when it comes to filling in forms. My boss is always complaining about silly errors and mistakes, which have caused problems for my company in the past. I try very hard to be accurate, but somehow seem to misread the instructions and make a muddle. I have no confidence in my ability in this area although I am otherwise very competent when tackling office duties.

Carol's Performance Analysis

Q: *What do I usually do wrong?*

Carol's first response was to say that she made a mess of every form she was ever given, left out important details, misread questions and failed to follow instructions!

After careful reflection, and by observing her performance while completing several forms during the analysis period, she realised that her errors occurred most frequently on two sorts of form: those which came from various government departments and those which required detailed numerical information. So her more considered answer to the first question was:

A: 'Make errors when writing down numbers. Misread instructions, and make many mistakes on official forms.'

Q: *What do I usually do right?*

Here again her first reaction was to believe that she rarely filled in any forms efficiently. But, after thinking about it, Carol concluded that she had little difficulty when completing forms on behalf of her two young children, or those filled out as part of her unpaid duties as social secretary to her local sports club.

A: 'Complete forms brought home from school by my children and those relating to sports club.'

The third question, *'What is distinctive about my failure?'*, was now easy to answer.

A: 'Occurs when completing official forms and those requiring numbers, especially when connected with my work.'

Q: *Where do I usually do it wrong?*

A: 'In the office during the normal working day.'

Q: *Where do I usually do it right?*

A: 'At home. At the sports club. In the office after the others have gone home.'

Her answers to the next three questions helped shed further light on her performance.

Q: *What's different about the places where I do it wrong?*

A: 'Busy work environment, versus relaxed, friendly, home surroundings.'

Q: *When do I usually do it wrong?*

A: 'While being observed by others whom I think know more than I do, are more competent or assertive and might be critical of my performance. When confronted by officialdom.'

Q: *When do I usually do it right?*

A: 'While working alone or with only family or friends around. When I know I have the answers at my fingertips. In social situations where officialdom is not involved. When completing forms for people I know. When not working with numbers.'

Q: *What's different about the circumstances when I do it right?*

A: 'I feel relaxed, not under critical scrutiny, knowledgeable and on top of the job, and have plenty of time to think about my answers without worrying that others are getting impatient.'

Q: *With whom or what is my failure usually associated?*

A: 'Numbers, officialdom, critical appraisal.'

Q: *With whom or what is my failure not usually associated?*

A: 'Non-official forms, those needing only word answers; those completed in a relaxed atmosphere away from critical scrutiny.'

Q: *How often do I fail?*

A: 'Frequently with official forms filled in against a tight deadline and/or under critical scrutiny, especially if numbers are involved.'

Q: *How often do I succeed?*

A: 'Almost always when the form is not an official one.'

Q: *What's different about these two situations?*

A: 'If I make a mistake in the office I feel foolish. My boss is very sarcastic about my carelessness. Errors involving numbers are easier for other people to spot. Figures cause me to feel confused and anxious so I am more likely to make a mistake with them than with words.'

Carol now understood that she mainly failed to perform as she wished when completing certain types of forms under particular conditions. She also knew that her mistakes increased where numbers were involved or when she filled out the answers while under critical scrutiny. The success she enjoyed when completing forms at home or in her role as club secretary showed that the majority of Carol's action programs for form filling were perfectly satisfactory. What let her down were management programs run under conditions of critical scrutiny. These produced unhelpfully high levels of arousal and mental confusion.

Carol also realised that many other aspects of her performance were undermined by the conditions which impaired her form-filling ability. Any critical comments or the risk of being seen to make a mistake served to reduce her confidence and increase anxiety. Thus the analysis helped her appreciate that mistakes made on forms were a symptom of more wide-ranging problems relating to her self-image, assertiveness, confidence, reaction to criticism and powers of concentration when under pressure.

The second case history which I am using to illustrate how differencing is used was completed by Philip, a 49-year-old divorced lawyer.

He described his problem as:

> Trying to make a favourable impression on women I find attractive. As soon as the conversation begins getting personal, I feel inadequate and try to sell myself so hard that I come over as aggressive and egotistical. Knowing what I am doing, but not knowing how to stop, I get so anxious and embarrassed that I have to walk away from the conversation. This failure to remain relaxed and not to try too hard to impress women has ruined many potential relationships in the past.

Philip's Performance Analysis

Q: *What do I usually do wrong?*

As with Carol, Philip's initial response to this question was to believe that he was unable to talk to attractive women about anything. A more detailed examination of this difficulty, and self-observation over a two-week period, revealed that his real difficulty was in getting serious about himself and his feelings, both towards himself and the woman he was with.

A: 'Become anxious and lacking in confidence when trying to have a serious conversation, especially with a woman I find attractive.'

Q: *What do I usually do right?*

A: 'Introduce myself. Have enjoyable but superficial conversations.'

Q: *What is distinctive about my failure?*

A: 'It only happens when I find myself wanting to make a strong impression. To force that woman, in a way, to like me and admire me.'

Q: *Where do I usually do it wrong?*

A: 'When meeting a woman on her own, either at my place or hers, or in some other intimate situation such as a quiet dinner for two.'

Q: *Where do I usually do it right?*

A: 'At parties or when lots of other people are around.'

Q: *What's different about the places where I do it wrong?*

A: 'The atmosphere is more intimate, there are less distractions and it's harder for me to change the subject and steer clear of serious topics.'

Q: *When do I usually do it wrong?*

A: 'When trying to talk about matters of importance to me, my feelings towards the woman especially.'

Q: *When do I usually do it right?*

A: 'While having casual conversations.'

Q: *What's different about the circumstances when I do it right?*

A: 'I am feeling relaxed and casual. I have a feeling that I shall be rejected.'

Q: *With whom or what is my failure associated?*

A: 'Women I find attractive and with whom I would like to have a relationship.'

Q: *With whom or what is my failure not associated?*

A: 'Friends, casual acquaintances.'

Q: *How often do I fail?*

A: 'Every time when hoping to develop a close relationship.'

Q: *How often do I succeed?*

A: 'Most of the time so long as the relationship is superficial.'

Q: *What's different about these two situations?*

A: 'I feel threatened at having to put my feelings into

words. I fear being hurt, rejected, or not being understood.'

After completing this analysis Philip was able to see that a major problem was not just his inability to express himself openly towards a woman for whom he felt a close attraction, but to discuss his true feelings with anyone.

The only conversations in which he felt secure were those sufficiently superficial to make the exchange of confidences unlikely. Philip realised that it would be necessary to explore his high-level management programs concerned with sharing deeply held feelings and confronting, rather than avoiding, painful emotions.

Mind-mapping

While differencing is an effective method for identifying the causes of failures once you are able to focus on a specific difficulty, it sometimes happens that you are rather unclear about what is going wrong and undermining your performance. To help clarify issues, prior to carrying out that type of analysis, you can explore the programs you bring to bear on any activity by mind-mapping the task.

How To Mind-map

1. Start by choosing some tasks which you perform on a fairly regular basis and where you would find it helpful to explore your performance in more detail. I suggest you select six for the first analysis. Some should be activities where you are usually satisfied with your performance, others those where you often fail to attain desired goals.

One of my clients, a 46-year-old bank executive, for example, chose: making presentations, chairing meetings and making financial decisions as three areas where he felt competent; and interviewing, reprimanding subordinates and playing in squash contests as three in which he was less satisfied with his performance.

A woman computer programer, who ran her own business from home, selected writing and debugging programs, as two of her best-performed tasks; swimming and helping her children with their homework as two where she was less satisfied with her performance; while cooking and driving the car were the tasks in which she considered herself least competent.

Having selected your six, start by choosing any one of them – it doesn't matter where you begin – and rate your performance on that activity against the twenty statements in Fig. 4.

Fig. 4 Mind-map

When carrying out this activity I am:

1. Stimulated   Bored
   +10 +9 +8 +7 +6 +5 +4 +3 +2 +1 0 −1 −2 −3 −4 −5 −6 −7 −8 −9 −10
2. Clear-thinking   Confused thinking
   +10 +9 +8 +7 +6 +5 +4 +3 +2 +1 0 −1 −2 −3 −4 −5 −6 −7 −8 −9 −10
3. Relaxed   Tense
   +10 +9 +8 +7 +6 +5 +4 +3 +2 +1 0 −1 −2 −3 −4 −5 −6 −7 −8 −9 −10
4. Decisive   Indecisive
   +10 +9 +8 +7 +6 +5 +4 +3 +2 +1 0 −1 −2 −3 −4 −5 −6 −7 −8 −9 −10
5. Confident   Uncertain
   +10 +9 +8 +7 +6 +5 +4 +3 +2 +1 0 −1 −2 −3 −4 −5 −6 −7 −8 −9 −10
6. Observant   Unobservant
   +10 +9 +8 +7 +6 +5 +4 +3 +2 +1 0 −1 −2 −3 −4 −5 −6 −7 −8 −9 −10
7. Consistent   Inconsistent
   +10 +9 +8 +7 +6 +5 +4 +3 +2 +1 0 −1 −2 −3 −4 −5 −6 −7 −8 −9 −10

8. Imaginative   Unimaginative
+10 +9 +8 +7 +6 +5 +4 +3 +2 +1 0 −1 −2 −3 −4 −5 −6 −7 −8 −9 −10

9. Persistent   Easily discouraged
+10 +9 +8 +7 +6 +5 +4 +3 +2 +1 0 −1 −2 −3 −4 −5 −6 −7 −8 −9 −10

10. Clever   Stupid
+10 +9 +8 +7 +6 +5 +4 +3 +2 +1 0 −1 −2 −3 −4 −5 −6 −7 −8 −9 −10

11. Fulfilled   Dissatisfied
+10 +9 +8 +7 +6 +5 +4 +3 +2 +1 0 −1 −2 −3 −4 −5 −6 −7 −8 −9 −10

12. Agile   Clumsy
+10 +9 +8 +7 +6 +5 +4 +3 +2 +1 0 −1 −2 −3 −4 −5 −6 −7 −8 −9 −10

13. Controlling   Controlled
+10 +9 +8 +7 +6 +5 +4 +3 +2 +1 0 −1 −2 −3 −4 −5 −6 −7 −8 −9 −10

14. Skilled   Unskilled
+10 +9 +8 +7 +6 +5 +4 +3 +2 +1 0 −1 −2 −3 −4 −5 −6 −7 −8 −9 −10

15. Involved   Indifferent
+10 +9 +8 +7 +6 +5 +4 +3 +2 +1 0 −1 −2 −3 −4 −5 −6 −7 −8 −9 −10

16. Energetic   Lethargic
+10 +9 +8 +7 +6 +5 +4 +3 +2 +1 0 −1 −2 −3 −4 −5 −6 −7 −8 −9 −10

17. Challenged   Threatened
+10 +9 +8 +7 +6 +5 +4 +3 +2 +1 0 −1 −2 −3 −4 −5 −6 −7 −8 −9 −10

18. Accurate   Inaccurate
+10 +9 +8 +7 +6 +5 +4 +3 +2 +1 0 −1 −2 −3 −4 −5 −6 −7 −8 −9 −10

19. Successful   Failure
+10 +9 +8 +7 +6 +5 +4 +3 +2 +1 0 −1 −2 −3 −4 −5 −6 −7 −8 −9 −10

20. Rational   Irrational
+10 +9 +8 +7 +6 +5 +4 +3 +2 +1 0 −1 −2 −3 −4 −5 −6 −7 −8 −9 −10

On Statement 1, for instance, you might rate an activity as +9 or even +10 if you found it highly stimulating, or −9 or −10 if totally lacking in stimulation. More often activities will be rated between the two extremes, indicating a degree of – for example – stimulation or boredom. Sometimes a statement will not be applicable to the activity you are evaluating, in which case it should be ignored.

Construct the mind-map using a grid similar to that illustrated (above). Copy this to avoid marking the book. Now create the map as follows:

Add your ratings for the odd- and even-numbered statements separately. This gives you two scores, which may be either positive or negative, for each activity.

On the mind-map, management program scores (i.e. totals on odd-numbered statements) are on the vertical line, with positive values above the horizontal line and negative values below it. Action program scores (i.e. totals on even-numbered statements) are located on the horizontal line, with positive values to the right of the vertical line and negative values to the left.

Your two scores enable you to map any activity in one of four zones, using exactly the same method as you adopt to locate a place on a map by using vertical and horizontal grid lines. If, for example, an activity scored +25 on action programs and −50 on management programs, it would be located at position A on the mind-map, as illustrated opposite. This is in the zone of uncertainty.

Each of the four zones is divided into three areas as shown overleaf.

If an activity is located in Section One, of any zone, the influence of both action and management programs will be low. This indicates that either the activity mapped is not especially important to you or that the statements provided are insufficiently relevant. In this case, I suggest you replace some of them with descriptions of your own, as explained later.

The following comments apply more strongly to activities in Section Two, and are highly relevant to those in Section Three of any of the four zones.

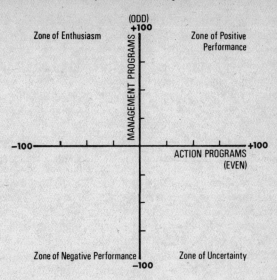

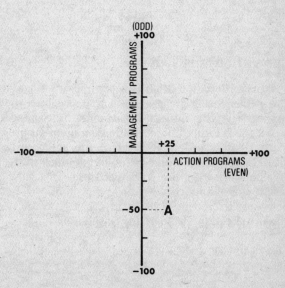

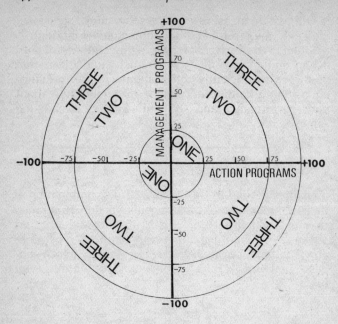

Zone of Enthusiasm

Here a combination of positive management and negative action programs suggests that the task may be approached with more enthusiasm than expertise. If an activity was located high on the management program (vertical) line and to the left of the action program (horizontal) line you may be fooling yourself into thinking that you are more competent than is actually the case.

Zone of Positive Performance

This is the most positive area of the grid and you will usually have placed an activity here only if you perform it with a fair measure of success on most occasions. However, be careful about getting overly confident. A position in the top right of the grid (high ratings for both action and management programs) could mean that you were insufficiently critical about your performance and ignoring failures. Try being more objective about your performance and see if the ratings remain the same.

Zone of Uncertainty

Activities located in this zone, with its combination of negative management and positive action programs, may be tackled with more skill than confidence and enthusiasm. Your action programs appear to be more efficient than your management programs, which suggests that unhelpful attitudes could be holding you back.

Zone of Negative Performance

An activity placed in this zone is likely to be performed poorly on most occasions, since key management and action programs have both been negatively rated. You will need to work on both these aspects of failure in order to increase success rates.

Where either management or action programs have received an overall negative rating, return to the statements and note down those negatively rated. Is there a common pattern to your lack of success on certain tasks? Do certain aspects of performance, such as being easily discouraged, feeling frustrated, or lacking confidence, appear across a range of activities? If they do then this pattern could provide important insights into the underlying causes of failure.

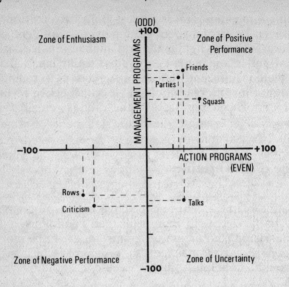

Mind-mapping in action

Let's consider a completed mind-map to see how this form of presentation assists in understanding how and why mistakes are occurring.

This map was made by Peter, a 36-year-old government employee. His chosen activities were: (successful) playing squash; giving parties; making friends; (unsuccessful) giving talks; family rows; responding to criticism.

Playing squash scored at even +50 and odd +48; giving parties was rated at even +30, odd +60. Making friends even +35, odd +70.

Two of the tasks on which he considered himself unsuccessful, family rows (even −60, odd −40) and responding to criticism (even −50, odd −50) had combined scores which placed them in the zone of negative performance. The final activity, giving talks, Peter rated at even +35 and odd −47, suggesting that he had a somewhat more negative attitude towards his ability than was justified by the level of skill brought to the task.

When Peter examined the rating statements on which he had scored himself negatively he discovered that activities where he felt successful were all rated positively on Statement 13 showing that he felt in control when he attempted them. The unsuccessful activities, by comparison, were negatively rated on this statement indicating that he experienced a loss of control while attempting them. They were also negatively rated on Statements 2 (clear-headed – confused); 3 (relaxed – tense); 5 (confident – uncertain); and 7 (consistent – inconsistent).

This suggested to him that feeling he was being controlled by events, rather than managing to exert control over what was going to happen, might be an underlying cause of his difficulties. He confirmed this by analysing the activity of greatest concern (responding to criticism) by means of differencing.

He then developed a reprograming schedule, based on the procedures described in Steps Four and Five to help him become more relaxed, confident and clearheaded when confronted by situations which denied him the chance to control events.

Creating Your Own Rating Scale

The twenty statements used for mind-mapping have been identified by my research as those most likely to influence performance over a wide range of activities.

But there is no reason why you should not create additional statements of your own, either adding to the list or replacing any which are inappropriate to your circumstances.

Remember that you should add statements in pairs, one relating to an action program and one to a management program, in order to maintain a balance between the two.

Mind-mapping and differencing offer powerful tools for clarifying one's thoughts about the positive and negative aspects of performance. They enable us to become more objective and, therefore, more insightful about our approach to any task. This helps us achieve a far better understanding of what we are doing right, as well as where and why things may be going wrong.

The more you use these self-assessments, the more easily you will be able to arrive at the heart of your difficulties as the first, essential, step to bringing about constructive change.

Continuing with the Training

After working with Steps One and Two for around three weeks, and when you have identified the aspect of your performance you want to improve, it is time to move to Step Four.

If your analysis revealed difficulties relating to any of the topics opposite, then you should start using the procedures described in the appropriate action plan, from Part Three of the book, simultaneously with moving on to Step Four.

Problem Area	Include In Your Training
Learning, studying, remembering, recalling information	Alpha Action-Plan One
Decision-making	Alpha Action-Plan Two
Problem-solving	Alpha Action-Plan Three
Stress management	Alpha Action-Plan Four
Physical fitness	Alpha Action-Plan Five

If your analysis revealed difficulties relating to any of the following:

learning, studying, remembering, recalling information
decision-making
problem-solving

then you should start using the appropriate Alpha Plan from Part Three of the book, simultaneously with moving on to Step Four.

Step Four: Mind-mirroring

Timetable

Start working with this procedure from about the third week of training.

Introduction

Ever since the nineteenth-century French therapist Emile Coué invented the self-improvement slogan 'Every day and in every way, I am becoming better and better', people have been attempting to enhance their performance through the power of positive speech. While this is fine in theory, Coué's advice has one major drawback: it rarely works. But then, when you think about it, there is no reason why it should!

Words alone, no matter how positive, are seldom sufficient to change long-established habits of thought and action. Spoken instructions of any kind have to be reinforced in many other ways if they are to establish new patterns of behaviour. The Chinese proverb, 'I hear and I forget; I see and I remember; I do and I understand', perfectly captures the reality of mastering new skills and adopting a different outlook on life.

However, the negative influence of words, especially when a particular comment is repeated often enough, must not be underestimated. They can act like an acid, slowly but surely eating away at confidence and ability until performance is so seriously weakened that the whole structure is in danger of collapse. This is especially likely to happen when the unhelpful remarks refer to some specific activity, such as remembering names, working with figures, or learning something new.

For this reason everything you say about yourself, even silently to yourself, must always be absolutely positive. Never allow yourself to make such comments as: 'I have a terrible memory for names . . .', 'I can't cope with figures . . .', 'I don't have a head for languages . . .', 'I'm hopeless when it comes to understanding anything technical . . .', 'I have no sense of direction . . .'. After only a few repetitions such negative statements can become part of a powerful management program which effectively closes the door to future attainment.

Acquiring Your New Programs

As I explained in Chapter Five, action and management programs are created as the brain organises a wide and varied range of incoming information. This includes everything seen and heard, tasted, touched and smelled as well as the way your body moved while performing physical actions. If new programs are to be used in preference to the older, more familiar ones, they have to be established in the brain using as many of these inputs as possible.

Furthermore, new instructions must always be precise; vague exhortations such as Coué's 'every day and in every way . . .' are far too general to influence such specific actions as playing sports, learning, problem-solving or decision-making. Giving your brain ambiguous commands of this kind is like telling a child to 'be good', without ever explaining what you mean by 'good' conduct. All instructions to the brain should be reasonable, reliable and realistic if they are to have any impact.

In this step of the training I will explain how you can use a procedure called mind-mirroring to practise any new programs in fantasy before attempting them in real life.

Your imagination, when trained and used correctly, provides a unique training ground in which to practise new behaviours that could prove too difficult, or too embarrassing, to attempt in reality. Through the employment of powerful mental images it becomes possible to create many versions of a particular situation, exploring the various attitudes you might wish to adopt, the remarks you might like to make and the probable responses of others within the privacy of your mind.

Mind-mirroring

The closest physical analogy to this Alpha-Plan procedure is the flight simulator used for training airline pilots to handle a wide range of emergencies, such as air stalls, wind sheers, and engine fires, without ever leaving the ground. The simulator enables the skills (action programs) needed to cope with dangerous situations to be perfected without any risk to those involved. It is the same with mind-mirroring.

The procedure itself is extremely simple. You just imagine yourself carrying out some activity in the way you would ideally like to perform it. After several rehearsals in fantasy, during which your mind mirrors external reality as accurately as possible, it becomes far easier to carry out that activity, with the same level of success, in real life. When sportsmen and women use this technique to improve their performance they may see themselves moving around a familiar course or race track, taking part in a highly competitive game, or recovering from an early blunder and going on to win.

The advantage of this form of visual rehearsal over

simply trying to remember what has happened or anticipate what could occur is that mind-mirroring usually proves a great deal more accurate. For example, after a professional skier was disqualified for falling during a race, he believed that his tumble had been due to a sudden change in snow conditions. When mind-mirroring the event, however, and asked to take special note of what had happened on the fateful turn, he realised that the faulty performance was due not to the snow but to placing his weight on the wrong ski at the turn. Having made this accurate diagnosis, the skier then used the same procedure to correct the error, first in his imagination and later in real life.

Many world-class athletes are now using mind-mirroring regularly in order to achieve consistently high performances. Three-times gold medallist skier Jean Claude Killy, reports that, because of an injury during practice, the only rehearsal he had for one event was to ski the course in his imagination. He regards that race as one of his best-ever performances. Golf champion Jack Nicklaus says that he imagines a ball landing on the green and sees it bounce. Next he visualises the arc of the ball in flight, his swing and finally the ball leaving the ground. He then joins these images together in the correct sequence: his swing, the ball's trajectory, its landing and bouncing on the green in order to achieve the perfect stroke. Chris Evert Lloyd focuses on images of her opponent's style and strategy, then visualises herself countering with an attack of her own.

One tennis player who had been beaten in 85 per cent of her games prior to visual-imagery training lost only one during the remainder of the season. A bowler raised his average from 185 before training to 215 afterwards, while a basket-ball player improved from shooting 61 per cent from the free-throw line and 38 per cent from the floor to 90 per cent and 50 per cent respectively.

But mind-mirroring is not just helpful when playing sports. Those attending Alpha-Plan workshops have also used it to help them enjoy greater success in such diverse activities as making friends to making love; passing exams and driving tests; losing weight; improving public speaking; handling aggressive clients; regaining self-confidence; controlling stress and attending interviews.

Like the other Alpha-Plan procedures mind-mirroring requires regular practice over a period of two or three weeks, and should be started only after you have learned to relax physically and are able to develop the receptive mental state associated with alpha production.

To use mind-mirroring to maximum effect, you first need to ensure that the fantasies you will be creating are as clear and vivid as possible.

Testing Your Mirroring Skills

By now you should be reasonably good at creating and sustaining the pleasant image of a sun-warmed beach which you have been using during physical relaxation.

Now the time has come to examine the strengths and weaknesses of that skill more closely. If you have followed the imaging procedure described in Step One you will have been forming an impression of the sun-warmed beach involving:

* *Sight* – picturing sun, sea and shore vividly.
* *Sound* – hearing the waves breaking gently on the beach.
* *Scent* – smelling the sea breeze and the flowers.
* *Touch* – feeling the sun on your body and the sand warm under your back.
* *Taste* – the tang of salt on your lips.

Before you read any further I would like you to go through a relaxation session and develop that tranquil, soothing scene as vividly as you can. Try to produce clear sensations of sight, sound, scent, touch and taste.

Hold that image for two or three minutes before returning from your relaxed state and immediately rating each aspect of that scene using the scale in Fig. 5. Once again I suggest that you note the ratings on a separate sheet of paper to avoid marking this book.

Start by considering your visual impression, then reflect on the clarity of any sounds. Next think about the sensations of scent, touch and taste. When you have finished, total your score for that scene.

Fig. 5 Mind-mirror – Analysis

Experience	Rating
As clear and as vivid as if I had actually been there	6
Very clear and almost as vivid as if I had actually been there	5
Fairly clear and vivid	4
Not very clear but some impression conveyed	3
Fleeting impression, neither clear nor vivid	2
No impression other than knowing I was thinking about that sensation	1

Few people achieve the maximum possible score of 30 points without training. A score of 20+ is extremely good and indicates that you have mastered the procedure well. Between 12 and 19 is an average score, while anything below 12 suggests that you are having difficulties with some, or all, of the imaging.

If your score was on the low side do not feel discouraged because the five exercises overleaf will allow you to develop this talent. If your score was average or above, then you have a good foundation on which to build. Concentrate especially on those aspects of the imagery where you found it especially hard to create realism.

In her book *Drawing on the Right Side of the Brain*, American psychologist and art teacher Betty Edwards asks why it is that the majority of adults have the drawing ability of a twelve-year-old child. The answer, she suggests, is that we lose the ability to 'see'. As she points out, 'contrary to popular opinion, manual skill is not a primary factor in drawing . . . *Seeing* is the problem, or, to be more specific, shifting to a *particular way of seeing.*' By this she means shifting from thinking dominated by the logical, left hemisphere of the brain to the more intuitive, and imaginative right hemisphere.

Training yourself to create mind mirrors involves getting in touch with your own sensations to a far greater extent than is normally achieved in today's world. This in itself is beneficial since, by looking and listening more clearly, by smelling, touching and tasting more vividly you can turn even mundane surroundings into rich sensory experiences.

The five exercises below involve listening, seeing smelling, touching and tasting with greater intensity than usual. I suggest that you start by working with those sensations which you found it hardest to recreate in your imagination. If all proved equally hard to conjure, then begin with improving your powers of visual imagery and then practise adding sounds to those sights.

Exercise One

Pay careful attention to everything you see. While doing so take as little notice as possible of information from your other senses. Study the whole before focusing in on details.

If you are in the country, for example, survey the

landscape as if seeing everything in it for the first time in your life. Notice how fields intersect, the way hedges, walls or fences follow the line of the countryside. Explore the shadows cast by trees and hedgerows. Absorb tones, shades, colours and hues. When you have done this for a while shift your gaze and examine with great attention to detail some particular aspect of your surroundings: the texture of bark, the way sunlight spills through leaves and dew on the grass.

If you are in a town or city, study the shape of buildings, examine the slant of roofs and the different textures of the walls. Notice displays in shop windows and the way passers-by are dressed. Make believe that you are a traveller from a country which lacks all buildings and traffic. Try and imagine how they would appear to you.

Exercise Two

Now switch from looking to listening. Explore the sounds as carefully and intently as possible.

Notice sounds at a distance and those close by. Observe how they change, blend and merge into one another. Focus all your attention on this input. If it is safe to do so, close your eyes to avoid distracting images. While listening in this way avoid labelling sounds. Instead of thinking, for instance, 'aicraft flying high overhead' or 'dog barking close by', merely allow your brain to register these noises and attend to their tonal quality and colour.

Exercise Three

Now focus on the scents and odours around you while paying as little attention as possible to anything else. Distinguish between the various smells in the air around you and concentrate not on attempting to identify and name them, but simply on experiencing them. Avoid value judgements such as 'that's pleasant' or 'how horrible': remain as neutral and non-judgemental as possible.

Although we may only become aware of them when especially pleasant or repugnant, smells frequently exert a profound influence over our behaviour, although we may remain quite unaware of their influence. They trigger memories and emotional responses without our realising exactly why we are recalling some event or experiencing a change of mood.

One reason for their potency is that, unlike information being sent from the eyes and ears, signals from the millions of odour detectors lining our nasal passages pass directly to the brain. Perhaps because of this, our memory for smells is more powerful than for most other information. Research by Trygg Engen of Brown University, for example, has shown that people can distinguish between odours smelled 30 days previously with 70 per cent accuracy. This compares with an accuracy of only about 10 per cent for visual and auditory information, over the same period.

So don't ignore your sense of smell during training. Skill in recalling the scents associated with a particular event will enhance both the realism of that scene and your recall of memories associated with it.

Exercise Four

Carry out this exercise the next time you are eating, sucking or chewing anything. Again it may help you to close your eyes as you focus on the different sensations produced. Notice not only the taste but also the changing texture and consistency of the food as you move it around in your mouth.

Taste and smell are, of course, very closely associated, although our olfactory system is around 25,000 times more sensitive than the sense of taste as judged by the concentrations which can be detected. In fact we are only able to recognise four taste sensations – salty, sweet, sour and bitter – by means of taste buds located primarily on the tongue. When we talk about the subtle taste of food, therefore, we are actually referring mainly to the odours released from the food, as a result of its being chewed, and detected by cells in the nasal cavities.

Including taste sensations in your mind-mirrors not only helps produce a more realistic fantasy, but can also be of positive advantage when creating some types of new programs. If you are trying to overcome anxieties caused by the thought of eating in public, for instance, (a fairly common phobic difficulty) then being able to taste the meal as you mind-mirror a dinner party will make it far easier for you to focus on the food, rather than any residual fears, when you reprogram in real life.

Exercise Five

Although you can carry out this exercise for enhancing the sense of touch almost anywhere, by focusing on signals from fingers and hands, there will clearly be certain situations in which these sensations are especially powerful: As you get into a hot bath or stand under a shower, for example, while walking barefoot through grass or over sand, when making a snowball with bare hands or stroking the coat of an animal and so on.

By carrying out these exercises regularly you will:

* Greatly enhance your powers of observation. Remember that incoming information is edited by programs which, when negative, may make you deaf and blind to many important aspects of your surroundings. This can all too easily distort reality, producing an impression not of things as they are but how we expect them or wish them to be.

* Provide a store of accurate memories that may be used for creating mind-mirrors.
* Sharpen your senses. Like everything else in the human body, these organs function best when used regularly. To keep sight, hearing, smell, taste and touch in prime condition they need to be exercised frequently.
* Improve your powers of concentration. This, in turn, will help enhance performance on virtually every mentally and physically demanding activity. Indeed the difference between a great thinker and a good thinker, or a supreme sports person and a merely high competent one, can often be found in their ability to concentrate completely on the job in hand.

When carrying out these exercises, bear the following points in mind:

1. Don't be surprised or disappointed if, at first, you find it difficult to concentrate on any single sensation since it is quite likely that unwanted thoughts will intrude. Should this happen simply notice that you have been distracted before returning to the exercise. After a while these intrusive ideas will gradually decrease until you are able to devote all your attention to the sense being trained.

2. Try not to categorise the sights, sounds, smells and so on as you attend to them. Merely notice them in as neutral a manner as possible.

3. Do not evaluate the information, at this stage, as pleasant or unpleasant, attractive or unattractive and so on. Just experience the sensation as objectively as you are able.

At first you can practise focusing on different sensations in various locations. But once you have gained some experience, the next task is to take just one scene – preferably somewhere you find relaxing and agreeable – and explore it thoroughly using each of the five senses in turn.

Then, during your next relaxation session, try to mind-mirror that scene as accurately as you can by drawing on the memories which you stored away during training. At the same time it is important not to become part of that mirroring, in the sense of watching yourself on a movie screen. You are not a character in the production but rather the creator of that scene, just as you would be if present in real life. In your mind see things through your eyes; hear through your ears; smell, taste and touch through your own nose, mouth and body.

After the exercise carry out another analysis using the rating scales provided. If you found it difficult to conjure up certain features of the scene, and this usually means for any part of the mirroring which achieved a clarity rating of three or less, return to the real-life scene as soon as possible and re-input all the data concentrating, of course, on those sensations which, although they formed an important part of the original scene, were poorly recalled during mirroring.

Mind-mirroring in action

The next stage in the Alpha Plan is to mind-mirror your performance when carrying out the activity on which you want to enjoy a greater level of success. To do this you must have a clear idea of the sort of performance you want to achieve as well as of any difficulties that are, currently, preventing you from enjoying success. When you've identified what's going wrong – using the procedures described in Step Three – write a short description of how you want to change your performance. By putting it down on paper you force yourself to define the difficulty clearly but concisely.

Of the three case histories which we considered in Step Three, Carol, with difficulties completing official forms, gave as her goal: 'being able to complete, confidently and accurately, complicated official forms, which require numerical information, when my boss is present'; Philip, who tried too hard to impress attractive women, wanted to 'remain relaxed and at ease during intimate conversations and not try to dominate the exchange'; Peter, who failed in situations where he felt himself unable to exert sufficient control over events, stated: 'staying calm and in command of myself when being criticised'.

Now proceed as follows:

1. Prepare the body by means of physical relaxation.
2. Prepare the mind, developing the alpha state.
3. Spend a few moments contemplating the soothing scene.
4. Switch your mind from the tranquil beach to a situation in which you confront your difficulty. You can, if you wish, recollect some actual occasion on which you failed to achieve the success you wanted and go over it again. Alternatively you can create a completely imaginary scene.

In either case, try to ensure that the mirroring remains as vivid as possible. Draw on your storehouse of sensations – sight, sound, touch, taste and smell – to devise a setting which is clear and detailed. During mind-mirroring act as you would ideally like to rather than the way you actually did – or consider you would be most likely to – behave.

Carol, for instance, pictured herself calmly and accurately completing a complicated official form, which required a lot of numerical information, while watched by her sarcastic boss. She started her mirroring by imagining entering his office and being handed the form with the instruction that it should be filled in as it had to be sent directly to a government department. She saw herself sitting down at the desk, and imagined the pressure of the seat beneath her body. Then she saw herself smoothing out the form and 'felt' the texture of the paper under her fingers. She mirrored the feel of the pen in her hand, and 'saw' the detailed notes on how to complete the form. She imagined reading those notes carefully, and not allowing anxiety to make her rush to respond until she fully understood what was needed. At one stage she even pictured her boss looking at his watch, and not allowing this show of impatience to stampede her into making silly errors. Finally she saw herself checking each section of the form carefully, correcting a couple of minor slips and then handing it to him for final approval.

When mind-mirroring:

* Be specific. You must see yourself carrying out some particular activity.
* Create images which are as vivid as you can make them. Use sights, sounds, taste, touch and smell.
* As I have already mentioned, live the part; do not observe that performance as though you were a detached observer watching yourself in action. You are the key player in this drama of the mind, not a member of the audience.
* If you start getting unduly anxious, switch scenes immediately and return to your tranquil beach. Spend a short while relaxing once again in order to eliminate unhelpful physical tensions. Go back into alpha and start again.
* If you are uncertain of exactly how you want to act in a particular situation, rehearse several different versions. You might be assertive in one and

less dominant in another, for example. Imagine how others present are likely to respond to your various approaches, and then consider your own responses to them.

At first you may find that your mind-mirror scenes are not very clear, or that they are hard to sustain. You may also start getting unhelpfully anxious almost as soon as you picture yourself in the stressful situation. But with a little practice you should find it perfectly possible to create and sustain powerful mirrors of real-life events. Furthermore, initial anxiety quickly declines with each repetition of the scene, allowing you to deal in a relaxed and confident manner with even the most stressful of challenges. When you do come to attempt them in reality this rehearsal will help you keep your fears under control.

Once you are able to cope confidently while mind-mirroring the time will have come to test out your newly established programs in the real world. How this may be achieved will be described in the final step of the Alpha Plan.

Step Five: The Alpha Plan in Action

Only start to practise in real life after you have carried out several sessions of mind-mirroring during which every aspect of the task, and your own response to it, have been thoroughly explored and you feel reasonably confident of being able to cope with it more successfully than in the past.

Introduction: If a job's worth doing . . . it's worth doing badly!

Perhaps that sounds like lousy advice. Yet failure, when viewed constructively, is the bedrock on which success arises. No task can ever be performed well unless it is first carried out badly.

Young children are usually very good at learning languages. Raise a child in a multilingual household and he, or she, will grow up speaking two, three, four . . . any number of languages. Psychologists used to believe that children succeeded where so many adults fail – just think how hard it seems to learn even a fairly straightforward language like French or German when you get older – because their brains were somehow different and special. Now it's recognised that the very young are not especially good at learning languages. Where they do excel is in making mistakes and then building on errors to produce success. They listen, they experiment, they blunder and they either get corrected or correct themselves by paying attention to the way other people speak.

As adults, errors make us anxious. We feel threatened, upset, distressed and diminished by them. When the language teacher corrects us each time we open our mouths it dents our ego, so we may abandon our studies to avoid the pain.

When you transfer any activity, successfully accomplished while mind-mirroring, into real life, I can guarantee one thing: you'll make mistakes. Even tasks which seemed relatively easy during mental rehearsal are going to prove more difficult in real life. You could find yourself still making some of the mistakes which undermined your performance in the past. So as you put the Alpha Plan into practice:

* Expect mistakes.
* Explore mistakes.
* Exploit mistakes.

Expect them because, while mind-mirroring is a powerful procedure which rapidly creates the rudiments of new programs in your brain, these fresh patterns of thought are far more tenuous and much less well established than the well-rehearsed programs you've got into the practice of using.

New programs are only able to exert their full effect over the things you say and do when they've been internalised: that is, once you have used them so frequently that the plateau of the learning curve illustrated on page 56 has been reached. Until that moment arrives, older, unhelpful but better learned programs will sometimes regain control. This means that set-backs and errors are almost inevitable. But don't worry about them. Used constructively mistakes will be friends not foes.

Explore failure by asking and answering these key questions:

What went right? Begin by being positive. Like the curate's egg, almost everything we do is good in parts. Think over the things you said, did or thought that proved effective, that increased confidence and skill, that improved performance. Reflect on any moments when you felt on top of the task. What was it about your thoughts, words or actions which produced that sense of self-assurance? Write these down under the (+) *this time* heading on the analysis form in Fig. 6.

Fig. 6 Performance Analysis

(+) *this time* Write down all the things you said, thought, or did that enhanced your performance	(+) *next time* Note positive aspects of your approach and use them both when mind-mirroring and in real life
(−) *this time* Write down all the things you said, thought, or did which undermined your performance	(−) *next time* Note negative aspects of your approach that must be overcome both when mind-mirroring and in real life

---

What lessons, general or specific, can you learn from them? Note these under (+) *next time* and include as many as possible when mind-mirroring or in real life.

What went wrong? Ask this question only when you've extracted all that was good from what was attempted. Some people embrace their failures with the eagerness of a masochistic monk donning a hair shirt. Never play the penitent because it produces more pain than gain. Be objective. Stand back from your performance; see it through the eyes of a detached observer. Ask yourself what you said, thought or did which increased anxiety, lowered morale, diminished performance.

But before focusing on supposed failures be sure they really were the mistakes you believe them to be. If possible get constructive feedback from people who witnessed your performance. They may have a totally different – and far more realistic – perception of the way you performed. Avoid asking people who are likely to respond with destructive criticism, sarcasm, point-scoring or – just as bad – mindless flattery. If you are the victim of cruel – and potentially destructive – comments try your best (and this is often easier said than done) to rise above them. Instead of considering them to be an accurate evaluation of what you have just said or done, see them for what they are, evidence that the critic is running some very negative – and ultimately self-destructive – programs of their own.

Later in this chapter I shall list the seven laws for creating effective programs. You can test other people's words and deeds against these just as easily as you can check your own. If they fail that assessment then you can be certain that the long-term loser will be whoever uses them against you. After Einstein fled to America from Nazi persecution, more than a dozen leading German physicists were ordered by their party bosses to sign an open letter declaring the theory of relativity to be nonsense. Following its publication Einstein was asked whether he had come to doubt his theory, since it had been repudiated by so many learned colleagues. With great dignity he replied that were his theory wrong it would require only *one* physicist to prove it wrong. A thousand can criticise and condemn without making you wrong. A thousand can compliment and concur without making you right.

The trouble is that we tend to be made so fearful by

our errors that we try not to think about them. As a result we are far more likely to stumble into the same trap on a future occasion.

Don't excuse your mistakes – exploit them. By building rather than brooding you can transform set-backs into successes.

Accentuate the Positive

Remember that our brainware evolves through the process of anticipation (as we predict the likely outcome of some activity); application (when we perform) and assessment (during which we review what was attempted and accomplished). For this reason it is essential to avoid acting, speaking or thinking negatively. Approaching any task in an apathetic and careless way, for instance, merely to get an unattractive chore out of the way, or muddling through instead of taking the necessary time and trouble to complete a job efficiently, will create programs extremely harmful to your overall success.

It is interesting how many religions, of both West and East, emphasise the importance of doing any job, however mundane and humble it may appear, to the very best of one's ability. A monk sweeping dust from the monastery floor, for instance, will attempt to do so as perfectly as possible and regard his task as no less significant than his companion who spends the day painting or writing. While it is rarely possible to invest routine chores with quite this degree of loving care in the bustle and tear of everyday life, one should always give of one's best in each and every major activity you undertake.

Striving for excellence in all aspects of your life is important not primarily because it may satisfy superiors, impress colleagues or set a good example for subordinates, nor because it can make your work more interesting and satisfying. The chief reward is that it helps to develop the positive management and action programs that lead to success across the whole spectrum of your activities.

For the same reason never comment on your talents or abilities in a negative manner. As I explained in Step Four, people who are constantly limiting their potential – 'I can't do that . . .' – or being dismissive about their abilities – 'I'm hopeless at this . . .' – are creating massively unhelpful management programs.

* You cannot *think* negatively without it adversely affecting your performance.
* You cannot *speak* negatively without it adversely affecting your performance.
* You cannot *act* negatively without it adversely affecting your performance.

The negative program spiral

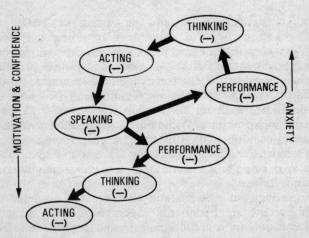

By contrast, positive thoughts, words and actions enhance all aspects of your performance.

The positive program spiral

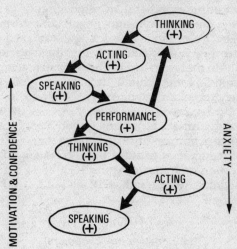

Management Programs Matter Most

Discussing the role of management in large companies, US business specialist Dr W. Edwards Deming, the man most credited with launching the renaissance of Japanese industry in the 1950s, comments: 'Problems in the system account for roughly 85 per cent of all productivity problems. Those are management problems.' His views are echoed by the chairman of McDonnell Douglas, the American aviation giant: 'When you get to the guts of what must be done you find that top management leadership is essential in the quality improvement process.'

Exactly the same degree of responsibility for the poor quality of an individual's performance can be attributed not to the brain's failure to acquire and use action programs, but to the acquisition of ineffective or downright destructive management programs.

I estimate that at least 75 per cent of all human failure is due to attitudes rather than either aptitude or ability. Change your outlook and you'll transform your prospects.

To do this you need to ensure that every action conforms to the seven laws of positive mental programming. Unless your actions do so, no performance, however excellent in itself, will prove to be of long-term benefit; instead of enhancing performance they must, eventually, undermine it. So once you have decided on a course of action, and before you put it into effect, ask yourself whether it satisfies these conditions. Only if you can honestly answer *yes* to each and every point should you go ahead and do it.

The Seven Laws of Peak Performance

Does what I propose:

1. Require me to take responsibility for what will be done and avoid unnecessary dependence on others? YES/NO.
2. Safeguard my legitimate rights without infringing the rights of others? YES/NO.
3. Arise from a constructive approach to life, and is not motivated by anger, envy, jealousy or revenge? YES/NO.
4. Express my true wishes and feelings? YES/NO.
5. Indicate neither a sense of inferiority nor superiority but of equality with others involved? YES/NO.
6. Enhance my own dignity and the dignity of others involved? YES/NO.
7. Involve an action which is both rational and compassionate? YES/NO.

Alpha Planning for Peak Performance

Success can be defined as the setting up and attainment of goals. Peak performance means achieving those goals as quickly and as efficiently as possible. To do this you must have a master plan, a chart which gives your journey through life direction and purpose. Without planning nothing can be achieved and the biocomputer cannot function effectively. Goals allow you to assign priorities in your life. This prevents wasted time and effort, and enables you to structure your days, weeks, months and years creatively.

Here is an exercise which, although it sounds slightly macabre, will help direct your mind to life goals of true significance to you. It involves writing out your own obituary by filling in the form below (as with previous forms it will be better to copy this on to a separate sheet of paper to avoid marking the book).

But this is an obituary with a difference. It will describe your accomplishments not as they are at this moment but as you would ideally wish them to be. It is a work of creative fiction in which your wildest dreams can be allowed to come true. So don't feel inhibited.

If you'd prefer to be remembered as a painter, deep-sea diver or the first paying passenger in space, then include that as an actual accomplishment in your mock obituary.

(*Your name*) died last night aged (*how old you'd like to be*) in (*where you would most like to live*). (*Your name*) worked as a (*the career you would most like to follow*) and reached the position of (*how high you hope to rise*). Away from work (*your name*)'s main interests were (*the hobbies, leisure interests you have or wish to have*). (*Your name*)'s many achievements included (*what you hope to accomplish*). (*Your name*) will be best remembered for (*what you are, or would be, proudest to accomplish*).

Now read through it again and identify key goals. Do these cover all aspects of a life – family, friendships, leisure interests etc. – or focus rather narrowly on just one – perhaps your career?

Next, complete the goal analysis chart below. Note every key goal and provide a short explanation of *why* each is important to you; and sort your goals, present and future, into the four major life areas.

Goal Analysis
Goal   *Why it is important to me*
Career   Present: Two years ahead: Ten years ahead: *Relationships*   Present: Two years ahead: Ten years ahead: *Personal*   Present: Two years ahead   Ten years ahead   *Leisure*   Two years ahead: Ten years ahead:

Take some time to devise a plan which will help you accomplish the goals sought in each of the four life areas. Keep this as simple as possible; half a sheet of paper is usually sufficient to develop the stages towards achieving a goal.

When creating your plan test each part of it by seeking answers to the following questions:

What am I attempting to do?
Why am I doing this?
How am I going to do it?
When am I going to do it?

What? The plan must be detailed – visualise each step along the way while mind-mirroring.

Why? Is this something you really want to do? A personally meaningful activity rather than one being attempted to please parents, boss, children, spouse, to impress the neighbours or to flatter a friend. Use the seven conditions for successful programming to check out the validity of your plan.

How? Have you considered the practical implications of what you propose? Think about costs – both financial and personal – and try to anticipate any snags which may arise. Be ready to exploit lucky breaks should they occur, but make certain that your plan doesn't depend on them. Each step must be within your capacity to carry through. If any are not, then break down your overall goal into a series of smaller, simpler, more easily attained, sub-goals.

When? Include a timetable in your plan. Know when you intend to start and when, approximately, you expect to finish. Be specific: 'One day I shall . . .' is no use at all. Remember: everything takes longer than anticipated – especially if it involves the co-operation or direct participation of others.

To accomplish any worthwhile plan you must develop management and action programs that provide you with the following qualities:

Vitality – in speech and action.

Courage – to overcome the inevitable disappointments, frustrations and set-backs.

Good humour – because cheerfulness sustains self-confidence and motivation while making it far more likely that others will co-operate with you.

Confidence – in your ability to attain your goals.

Thoroughness – so that every important aspect is considered and dealt with.

Firmness – to ensure control over yourself and others.

Sensitivity – to the effects of your plans on the lives of others.

These are far more likely to be present when your plan

* Makes you happy.
* Does not conflict with deeply held personal beliefs.
* Involves activities which help others – not only to yourself.
* Takes the interests and feelings of others (family/friends/colleagues etc.) into account.

Be clear that Alpha Plans do *not* involve:

* Striving after unrealistic goals.
* Being obsessively perfectionist.
* Trying to avoid ever making mistakes.
* Repeating the same activity over and over again until it can be done faultlessly.
* Avoiding unfamiliar tasks because you may perform below par.
* Refusing to compete for fear of being seen to fail.
* Over-investing time and effort in one project to the detriment of other areas in your life.

* Expressing constant dissatisfaction with your attainments.
* Being hypercritical of achievements – your own or other people's.
* Putting things off until you can do them perfectly.

In fact the Alpha Plan is just the opposite of all of these, as the following ten golden rules for peak performance clearly demonstrate.

The Golden Rules for Peak Performance

1. Life is for living and for getting things done. Build castles in the air if you wish – but never try to take up residence in them. Be a *doer and a dreamer*.
2. Every task is performed for a purpose. Alpha Planning is a means of achieving that purpose as efficiently and as speedily as possible. This applies whether the task is vitally important or essentially insignificant. Do not procrastinate – *get going*.
3. Creativity and successful problem-solving arise from actions as much as from thinking. When you get an idea, *try it*.
4. If a job's worth doing it's worth doing badly! No performance is perfect at first. You always improve with practice. *Make a start*.
5. Mistakes often tell you far more about your performance and how to improve it than successes. Do not try to avoid making them – *welcome mistakes*.
6. Never become too emotionally involved in a task – it inhibits performance. Be enthusiastic, caring and conscientious but *remain objective*.
7. When you have completed a task to the best of your ability, leave it. *Keep moving along*.
8. Avoid spending too much time reflecting on earlier successes. Be present-orientated. Learn from

previous achievements and use past triumphs to help plan for future achievements. *Live in the now.*

9. Never assume that because considerable time and effort have been expended on a task that the performance must be optimal. It is the efficiency with which that time and effort have been used rather than the actual investment of either that matters. See through the surface glister and *assess analytically.*

10. If you wait until you know *all* the facts you will probably never get started at all. Be prepared to take a chance. You will learn as you go along and, even more important, you will begin to see more clearly exactly what it is you most need to know. *Be biased for action* in your life.

Reviewing The Concepts

I'll conclude by summarising the key ideas behind the Alpha Plan, concepts which enhance our understanding of how it is possible to improve all aspects of performance by means of the plan's readily mastered procedures.

* The human brain is a biological computer which operates continuously, and simultaneously performs millions of computations. It is the most complex and highly organised structure in the known universe.
* The human brain is a general-purpose biocomputer which is capable of dealing with a tremendous range of problems varying greatly in their complexity. This is only possible because the hardware constantly modifies its own functioning through the creation of new software.
* There are two types of brainware: programs which accomplish the how of behaviour by allowing us to

do things (action programs) and those which regulate the where, when and why of behaviour (management programs).

* High-level programs influence those beneath them and are, in turn, modified and influenced by the outcome of the programs they run, through the processes of feedback and feedforward.

* Programs written into the genetic code establish the upper and lower limits of performance throughout life. However, the biocomputer's potential so far exceeds anything demanded of it – even by the world's greatest thinkers – that, except in the case of severe brain damage, these innate limitations are of no practical significance.

* The vast majority of programs are acquired by learning and vary in permanence. Some seem to be fairly short-lived and can be completely erased; others operate throughout life.

* New programs can be established and earlier ones modified throughout life. However, the majority of people fail to take advantage of this fact, and continue to operate programs developed early in life – during their formative years – long after they have ceased to work efficiently.

* In a rapidly changing world it is essential constantly to modify and to update action and management programs.

* Alpha Planning enables you to bring about this positive mental programming quickly and efficiently. By learning the skills of physical relaxation, alpha production, performance analysis, mind-mirroring, and real-life practice you will find it far easier to confront life's challenges and enjoy peak performance in all you do.

PART THREE

'When the only tool you have is a hammer, you tend to treat everything as if it were a nail.'

Dr Abraham Maslow

Alpha Action Plan One: Learning

> 'We don't know one millionth of one per cent about anything.'
>
> Thomas Edison

It has been estimated that about 50 per cent of everything we now know was learned before we reached the age of five. By the time we reach early adulthood, our brain has already stored more information than could be contained in all the millions of books in the British Library. The trouble is that most of the time we aren't able to gain access to it. For the problem with learning is not so much one of putting facts and figures into mental storage as of locating them again.

The secret of Alpha-Plan learning is to retain new information in such a way that it can be rapidly and reliably recalled to mind when the need arises.

Alpha-Plan Learning

It is ironic that although we spend most of our lives learning, either directly or indirectly, we are rarely taught how to learn easily and efficiently. Some people are fortunate enough to develop effective action programs for themselves and so find learning fairly easy. Others, having failed to do so, conclude that their brains can't meet the challenge of acquiring new knowledge and skills. As we have seen, this leads to the creation of negative management programs through the twin processes of feedforward and feedback.

What one needs are action programs which will ensure that learning is fast and efficient so that new knowledge and skills can be perfected in the least amount of time and with as little expenditure of effort and energy as possible. This is, in fact, the way that geniuses frequently work. They break down everything that needs to be learned into a number of topics which can be mastered one at a time. They have the ability to see a pattern in all learning tasks, whether it involves speaking another language or writing a computer program.

Alpha-Plan learning involves three separate tasks:

1. Information selection: choosing the things you need to know in order to do what is required.
2. Information structuring: organising items of knowledge in such a way that they can be learned most efficiently.
3. Information storage: transferring information from books, notes, film, audio cassettes, video tapes and so on into long-term memory.

Many people waste effort and energy by filling their heads with facts they rarely need to use and could just as easily look up when necessary. Einstein, for instance, never bothered to remember his telephone number because he felt that doing so was too trivial a use of brain power.

In all this you should be guided by your *purpose* in learning. Before starting to study anything new, ask yourself these questions:

Why do I need to learn this?
What goals can I achieve using this new knowledge or skill?

How can I use it?
When do I need to know it by?

Your learning purpose will often be more easily identified if you have worked through the goal-setting exercise described in Step Five of the Alpha Plan.

Information Selection

Start by deciding exactly what must be learned in order to accomplish the things you are setting out to achieve. Since your time is limited, but the demands on your time are virtually unlimited, learning too much is as inefficient as learning too little. Ask yourself what facts and figures have to be stored in your brain, because you'll need immediate access to those facts in order to solve problems or make decisions, and which can be more conveniently stored in files, notes, books and so on.

Information Structuring

Once you have decided what you must learn, the second step is to identify the information sources. When following a course of supervised studying this task is often done for you by the lecturers, who provide reading lists, suggest suitable reference sources and set down a timetable for acquiring different topics.

If you are studying on your own, make sure that your sources of information are as reliable and recent as possible. In many fast changing fields, such as computer science or biotechnology for instance, it is important to work from only the most up-to-date material to avoid acquiring obsolete, and possibly incorrect, knowledge.

Having decided on your reference sources, glance through these briefly to find out what material they contain. From this rapid scanning it should be possible to construct an overall learning plan. This should be sufficiently detailed for you to break down the subject-matter into a number of related topics.

If you were learning photography, for example, suitable topics might be:

Exposure of black-and-white and colour film
The use of lenses with different focal lengths
Using flash indoors and out
Developing black-and-white films
Processing colour films
Making black-and-white prints

Now choose one topic and extract as much information as you can from your different references. These will then be organised in such a way that every fact and figure can be added to what is called the brain's knowledge network. Because this is such a key concept in learning, we should look in more detail at just what this network is and how it makes memory possible.

Your Knowledge Network In Action

You have first-hand experience of your knowledge network at work each time you attempt, without success, to recall a familiar name or bring to mind a favourite quotation. Frequently it is only once the struggle has been abandoned, and you've turned your attention to some other task, that the elusive information suddenly pops, unbidden it seems, into your mind.

This happens because as the brain instructs the memory to track down some fact or figure, a search of the knowledge network is initiated. The hunt continues until the memory bank has been thoroughly investigated. But because the brain works under such pressure, one cannot afford to invest much time in a conscious search. So you turn your mind to other tasks, usually unaware that the memory is still being searched in accordance with the earlier instruction. Because the brain is under much less pressure at night the search can be made more rapidly; which is why sleeping on a problem often means waking up with an answer.

Immediately before coming up with the correct information, you may have noticed that you are likely to remember items which are related to, or similar to, the facts being sought. The name wanted is Jones; the name that comes to mind is James. This happens because the section of the network in which Jones is stored also contains names with a similar sound and/or spelling.

Learning and the Knowledge Network

Imagine the chaos if a careless librarian replaced books on the shelves of a billion-volume library at random. While none of those books could be said to have been lost, discovering the one you wanted to read would depend on luck rather than logic. Filling your memory with new information in a similarly haphazard manner creates exactly the same sorts of problems. Fast, accurate recall demands the same methodical approach one would adopt when placing titles on shelves or files in a filing cabinet.

You can prove this for yourself by reading the list, below, just *once* before attempting to write down the ten words – in the right order – from memory. If that's too easy write the list out for a second time, this time in reverse order.

Elephant. Umbrella. Bicycle. Hamster. Bus. Puppet. Ice-cream. Lighthouse. Frog. Church organ.

Don't feel bad if you were only able to recall a few of those words, or found it impossible to get them in the right sequence. Your failure does not mean that you've got a terrible memory; only that you are not, at present, using it properly.

By learning how to create a knowledge network you will discover that it is perfectly easy to bring to mind all twelve words, in the right sequence – even days later. What's more, you'll find it just as easy to write the list in reverse order or to start and finish at any point you choose.

Read through that list for a second time. On this occasion, instead of attempting to remember the words, transform each of them into a mental image, the crazier the better, before linking the various pictures to produce a mind movie.

You could, for example, imagine a huge, pink elephant holding a giant, striped, beach umbrella in its trunk whilst riding an antique bicycle. The elephant swerves to avoid a giant hamster, absent-mindedly crossing the street. The startled hamster jumps aboard a bus, which is being driven by a strange-looking puppet. The puppet, who is licking a giant ice-cream cone, stops the bus outside a tall lighthouse with a brilliantly flashing lamp. Peering through the lighthouse window you see a large, smartly uniformed, frog playing an ancient church organ whose bellows are being pumped by a sweating elephant.

It may sound like Salvador Dali's latest nightmare, but if you have imagined those pictures as I described them you'll be surprised at how easily each of the words can be recalled merely by replaying your mind movie. As each of those mad mental snapshots flashes into your mind, you will find that every object is recalled quickly, clearly and correctly. To produce the list in reverse order merely rewind the film, starting with the image of the church organ.

You'll notice that I associated the first word, 'elephant', with the last, 'church organ'. By doing so a list is transformed into a continuous loop so that it's possible to begin anywhere and proceed either forwards or backwards with ease. Prove how powerful this method is for yourself by memorising the list below:

Dog. Sky-diver. Island. Tent. Television. Bed. Military band. Coffee cup. Liner. Clown.

Remember to make the images as bizarre as possible, to link each one to its neighbour and to connect the first and last items to turn the list into a loop. Images are remembered where words may be forgotten because each of those familiar nouns is already in your memory store. However, since there are no direct associations between them, recalling one does not instantly bring the next to mind. The creation of unique images – did you have a picture of a pink elephant with an umbrella in your mind store before this exercise? – ensures that you fill your mental storehouse with new, and remarkable, memories. These are then joined together, producing a tiny addition to your brain's already vast and vastly complex knowledge network.

This provides the clue as to how you should structure knowledge in order to remember it easily and to recall it quickly and correctly. Rather than sitting down, wrapping your head in a damp towel and slogging your way through page after page of text, extract the required facts and jot down notes on a large sheet of paper – the A3 size is most convenient. None of the notes should be more than thirty words long; and when possible augment them with small drawings, doodles, or thumbnail sketches which illustrate key points. Read the notes aloud as you jot them down.

Next draw a circle around each item and join them together by lines which link each item to its neighbour in a logical way. Make certain that every fact is joined to two others, so turning the list into a loop. The way this might be done when studying photography is shown opposite:

No single sheet should contain more than twenty-five items, or it starts getting too complex and messy, which means you will need many such sheets for any complicated learning task.

As you probably realise, what you've done here is very similar to the procedure used for learning those ten words listed above. By linking all the items together on paper, you associated them in your mind in the same way. This means that you can begin anywhere on the loop, move in either direction and return to your starting fact after recalling every item. What's more, remembering just one item will bring to mind all the remainder.

Once the information has been extracted and organised in this way, you are ready to proceed to the third and final step of storing that knowledge in your brain.

Information Storage

Your knowledge network contains not only words, but memories of images, sounds, smells, and tastes as well as sensations of touch and movement. This means that triggering one memory often evokes a vast number of others. The smell of wild flowers, for instance, might bring to mind an apparently long-lost memory of a happy childhood excursion to the countryside.

If you think about the way you might approach spelling an unfamiliar word, you'll get a sense of how this multiple memory works. The first thing you might do is reach for pencil and paper and try writing down various versions of the word. At the same time you might think about the sounds involved in the word and recall the way certain sounds are spelled.

Here you are searching for the correct spelling by

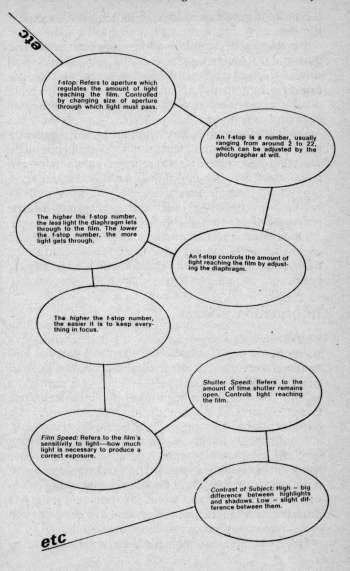

etc

f-stop: Refers to aperture which regulates the amount of light reaching the film. Controlled by changing size of aperture through which light must pass.

An f-stop is a number, usually ranging from around 2 to 22, which can be adjusted by the photographer at will.

The *higher* the f-stop number, the *less* light the diaphragm lets through to the film. The *lower* the f-stop number, the more light gets through.

An f-stop controls the amount of light reaching the film by adjusting the diaphragm.

The *higher* the f-stop number, the easier it is to keep everything in focus.

Shutter Speed: Refers to the amount of time shutter remains open. Controls light reaching the film.

Film Speed: Refers to the film's sensitivity to light—how much light is necessary to produce a correct exposure.

Contrast of Subject: High = big difference between highlights and shadows. Low = slight difference between them.

etc

reference to visual memories (by looking at the word on the page), sound memories (by repeating the word either silently or out loud), and muscle memories (also by writing it down). Your brain has stored away the series of commands which have to be sent to the muscles of the arms, hand and fingers in order to create the unique sequence of movements represented by each and every word.

While learning, therefore, store new knowledge in as many different memory locations as possible, in exactly the same way that you created mind-mirrors when in alpha using sight, sound, smell, taste and touch.

* Visualise it – make your mental pictures as bizarre as possible. This also helps to stimulate the right side of the brain, the hemisphere more concerned with images than words.
* Voice it – repeat the information silently or aloud. Record the information on tape and then replay it while reading the notes.

Whenever possible plug the ideas into taste, touch and smell memories as well.

Before starting to learn the items on a knowledge-network card, carry out rapid relaxation and go into alpha creation.

Now move around the loop of facts *twice*. It doesn't matter where you start.

Next cover all but one of the facts, read that item and attempt to recall the one either above or below it on the loop. Move in any direction you wish around the network, but having started you should continue in the same way until you arrive back at the starting point. If you get stuck, never try and force yourself to remember since this takes mind and body out of the learning state and into a condition of unhelpfully high arousal.

Stay physically and mentally relaxed. Free associate

by thinking of the first thing which the information just read brings to mind. This often provides the required clue. If you are really stuck, uncover and glance briefly at the next item so as to allow yourself a glimpse of those elusive facts. This is often sufficient for you to recall the information correctly. If you are still unable to remember, simply read it aloud again.

Continue in this way until you have moved around the network and recalled all the facts it contains. After just a couple of circuits you should find it easy to remember everything on the sheet. Once the information on a sheet has been learned, store it away carefully for revision purposes at a later date. But before starting work with another topic, allow yourself a break of at least 5 minutes in order to prevent one learning task from interfering with the next; no learning sessions should last longer than 20 minutes.

In order to establish the newly learned information firmly in your memory, go back over it a number of times the same day by having brief rehearsal sessions. Research suggests that the secret of success here is the manner and timing of these rehearsals.

One hour after learning a particular topic, relax, go into alpha and work around the loop of facts. Do not worry if you appear to have forgotten several of them. Simply try and recall what the last fact you remember reminds you of, remain relaxed and mentally tranquil as you did when learning the information. Never put pressure on the memory since this only arouses anxiety and interferes with intellectual performance.

Have a second recall session 3 hours after the first learning session, and a final rehearsal 6 hours later, or just before you go to sleep. This clear memory can then be maintained from then on with just an occasional rehearsal.

Action Program for Names

One of the most common complaints people make about their memories is that they can never remember people's names. This difficulty occurs primarily because that information is never properly memorised in the first place. While being introduced to somebody for the first time, the majority of people are so concerned about making a good impression that they fail to pay sufficient attention to details – names, titles, occupations and so on.

At the first meeting, listen carefully and then strengthen that memory by using the name several times during the first few minutes of conversation. If the name is an unusual one, be sure to check pronunciation and, perhaps, spelling before committing it to memory. While chatting, observe the other person's features carefully to pin-point any distinguishing characteristics, such as arched eyebrows, larger than average ears, high cheek bones, and so on.

Use these details to construct a mind-mirror caricature in which they are emphasised. That done, link your mind picture to the name – and any other relevant details about that person it might be useful to recall at a later date – in one of two ways. Either see it written – in bright red ink – on a white card placed below the face, as in police mug shots of criminals. Alternatively, and this is very helpful with unusual surnames, create a mind-mirror image based on that name. With a certain amount of ingenuity this is nearly always possible. A Mr John Launch, for example, could be imagined launching a boat with John painted on the side. To link further information to this image expand your memory movie to include these additional facts. If John is a scientist who collects antique furniture, picture his boat fitted out as a laboratory filled with ancient tables and chairs.

Summary of Alpha-Plan learning

* Start by deciding on your learning purpose. This tells you what you need to know and how much must be learned.
* Only try to remember information to which you will need immediate access when solving problems or making decisions.
* Organise information logically, make short notes and link these items into a logical structure so that facts are in the form of a loop rather than a list. Use drawings and doodles to stimulate the right side of the brain.
* Remember by creating as many memories as possible, through seeing, hearing, and where possible tasting, touching and smelling as well.
* When mind-mirroring, make your images as bizarre as possible.
* Relax and go into alpha before each learning session. Never strain after an elusive fact, it will come to mind more readily if you remain relaxed.
* Rehearse newly learned information a number of times on the same day.
* For successful learning it is important that the activity is personally meaningful to you. Try to change either the task itself and/or your attitude towards it so as to make it as relevant as possible.
* Try and learn something new every day. Like muscles, the memory needs to be exercised regularly in order to remain in peak condition.

Alpha Action-Plan Two: Decision-Making

'Between two evils, I always choose the one I haven't tried before.'

Mae West

A decision is a conclusion or a judgement. It's what happens when you make up your mind. Economist Andrew Leigh says:

> A decision implies . . . at least two or more possible outcomes, some kind of importance or value attached to these outcomes and variations in the effectiveness of the outcomes. These variations are what make the choice difficult and lead to the necessity to evaluate the alternatives carefully.

Nobody is immune from poor decision-making. Mark Twain, for example, went bankrupt after investing $250,000 in a company whose typesetting machine was so incompetently designed that it made setting type more rather than less complicated. At the same time he turned down an invitation to invest $5,000 in the new telephone company being set up by Alexander Graham Bell. Even Phineas T. Barnum, the showman who once proclaimed 'There's a sucker born every minute', went broke after deciding to invest in the Jerome Clock Company which turned out to be a swindle. It's easy to sympathise with President Warren Harding who, while struggling with a major domestic crisis, remarked to a friend:

> John, I can't make a damn thing out of this tax problem. I listen to one side and they seem right, and then, God! I talk to the other side and they seem just as right, and there I am where I started. I know somewhere there is a book that would give me the truth, but hell, I couldn't read the book. I know somewhere there is an economist who knows the truth, but I don't know where to find him and haven't the sense to know him and trust him when I do find him. God, what a job!

One of the problems is that, even when the choice is relatively limited and straightforward, we can never consider every possible option. To take an everyday example: you arrive at work and are faced with the task of deciding the best order to tackle ten office chores at the start of the working day. You have letters to write, phone calls to make, clients to see, a meeting to arrange, etc: in all ten different jobs which must be completed by five o'clock. The sequence in which you tackle them is important since if you leave letter-writing too late you'll miss the post, while calls made early will involve extra cost. Suppose that, being extremely methodical, you decide to work through every possible arrangement of those ten tasks in turn. Studies have shown that the human brain can do this fairly rapidly, and it should be possible for you to consider one alternative in twenty milliseconds. The trouble with this approach is that, even at that speed, it will require twenty hours to complete the task!

The only way to prevent ourselves from becoming paralysed by indecision, is to exclude a vast range of possible choices whenever we need to make up our minds. In the example, as soon as it was clear that letters had to be written early in the day, one would obviously reject all options which placed writing letters last in the list. Doing so immediately eliminates some 400,000 possibilities! Successful decision-making depends as much on what we ignore as what we consider when arriving at our final course of action.

We make so many decisions every waking moment of our lives that choosing becomes more a matter of habit than of careful thought, which is where the problems arise, since many of these habits are either inefficient or downright destructive.

An obvious danger is the snap judgement, where we decide rapidly and, often, thoughtlessly, in order to get the business of deciding over and done with as rapidly as possible. In his book *The Art of Decision-making*, Massachusetts business adviser John Arnold explains:

> Getting the decision behind us becomes more important than making sure the decision is a good one. We might just as well flip a coin. And some of us do the opposite. We worry ourselves sick over a decision but put off coming to any conclusion. Or we ask the advice of a friend. Unable to make a decision ourselves, we seek to share responsibility with others.

Yet decision-making is tremendously important since it is the skill which shapes our destiny. Each time we decide we learn a little more about the kind of person we really are, because choosing reflects our priorities and values.

Five Questions to Ask

You can avoid blunders in your decision-making by asking yourself these five questions prior to taking any action:

* Is my decision really necessary?
* Is there too much wishful thinking in my choice?
* Is every option being explored?
* Is it really my own decision?
* Does my decision depend too much on luck?

Is My Decision Really Necessary?

Asking yourself this basic, yet seldom raised, question can save a great deal of effort and expense. For instance, consider a couple's decision to refurnish their living room. Rather than spending their time wondering *how* to find the money, they should start by asking *why* they want new furnishings in the first place. If the answer is because their son has never brought his girlfriend home, they should ask whether he is embarrassed by the furnishings or just doesn't want her to meet his family. It could be that the real problem lies in family relationships rather than the furnishings.

Start by analysing the situation and circumstances surrounding your decision as carefully and as objectively as possible. Beware of defining your purpose too narrowly, of becoming trapped into an unnecessary decision through tunnel vision. Ask *why* before asking *how* and you may quickly realise that the best decision you can make is not to make any decision at all.

Is There Too Much Wishful Thinking In My Choice?

Many faulty decisions arise because people depend on wishing and hoping rather than knowing and understanding. Often there is a reluctance to confront the realities of the situation for fear of making oneself anxious or depressed, of lowering morale or undermining confidence. All too often those who attempt to draw attention to facts which others would rather ignore become accused of negative thinking and may find themselves ignored or unemployed. No matter how painful the short-term consequences may prove, however, it's far better to face up to the truth than live in a fool's paradise. A sign in the chairman's office of Braun, AG, offers this cautionary advice to company decision-makers: 'Entering a new business is easy and cheap; getting out is difficult and expensive.'

Never underestimate the importance of taking a long, hard, look at the evidence on which any decisions you must make are based.

Is Every Option Being Explored?

To make successful decisions it is essential to explore a wide range of options. Rather than being guided in your choice by a single, intermediate goal – the process often employed by poor decision-makers – learn to view the subject from many different perspectives. Ask yourself what is likely to happen, as a result of different options, not one, but two or more steps down the road.

The trouble is that as children we were more often praised for having a logical mind than a lively one. Because schools, and many homes, tend to regard correct solutions as being more valuable than original answers, we learn to channel our thoughts along acceptable lines – which almost inevitably means straight and narrow lines.

Such reasoning is dangerous because it often blinds one to all but the glaringly obvious. So before short-listing possible courses of action you need to make sure that all your choices have been thoroughly investigated.

You can do this most easily by taking a large piece of paper and noting down every idea that comes to mind, starting with obvious options and then proceeding to solutions which are more and more imaginative.

While doing this take the brake off your brain and allow your mind to run riot. Avoid the temptation of imposing rules or censuring your creative process. Be as silly as you like in your thinking. The actions you come up with should be adventurous rather than immediately practicable. It doesn't even matter if they seem a little crazy at first glance. Remember that some of the world's greatest discoveries began life as seemingly madcap schemes. Jot down every thought that comes into your mind. Link associated concepts by drawing in arrows. Only when you've finally exhausted your store of ideas should you stop being creative and start being critical.

Edit the choices by discarding any which are either completely impossible or totally impracticable. But be careful not to throw out any ideas until you have given each a fair trial. Sometimes a course of action which seems hopeless at first sight can be transformed into a practical reality with some further thought and modification.

Is It Really My Decision?

When making a decision be very sure that the choice is yours rather than someone else's. Try to avoid getting talked into some course of action you feel badly about, or talked out of doing something that you are sure in your heart is right. 'It's important to listen to other points of view and consider all the facts of an issue,' comments Dr Gary Emery, director of the Los Angeles Center for Cognitive Therapy. 'But letting others think for you is a poor way of making decisions. Efficiency always drops when you ask others to interpret the world for you.'

A classic example of the dangers which can arise when decisions are made by many people, rather than a single individual, is the 'risky shift'. This was first identified as one of the hidden hazards of decision-making in the 1960s, by Dr James Stoner of the Massachusetts Institute of Technology. In his studies, subjects were asked to make individual decisions about what should be done to imaginary characters in various stories. A variety of actions were suggested and these varied in terms of the amount of risk or reward involved. In each case, however, the greater the reward the higher was its associated risk. After making their decisions alone, the volunteers were brought together to decide, as a group, to make similar decisions for the same characters in the same situations.

When reaching decisions on their own, most volunteers picked middle of the road options which combined modest risks with moderate rewards. As a group, however, their judgements shifted in the direction of greater risk. James Stoner reported that the collective choice almost always involved the greatest gamble, with decisions ranging from the slightly rash to the downright foolhardy. This movement towards collective irresponsibility was termed the 'risky shift', and it dispelled once and for all the cherished belief that committees were more conservative in their judgements than the individuals who comprise them.

Listen to others, and take their views, ideas, beliefs, interests and assumptions into account when reaching your decision, but always be certain that the course of action finally adopted is what you feel is for the best, rather than a choice forced on you by others.

Does My Decision Depend Too Much On Luck?

You've been betting on the toss of a coin and it's come down heads a staggering twenty times. The next time it is bound to be tails, just on the law of averages, right?

Wrong, and if you believe otherwise you've fallen for one of the most frequently encountered hidden hazards of decision-making – gambler's fallacy. So long as no deception is involved, a coin can land heads a million times, without changing the 50/50 probability of it coming down either heads or tails on the millionth and first toss.

Gambler's fallacy is the belief that the past occurrence of an event always changes the odds of it happening again. It can happen of course, especially where human behaviour is concerned because, unlike coins, people have memories and learn from past mistakes. All the same, gambler's fallacy is the basis of more bad choices than almost any other single source of faulty decision-making. Take the case of a businessman who tells himself, 'I've lost money on the last four projects so I'm due for some luck on this one', or the three times married divorcee who tells herself, 'I'm bound to be lucky with husband number four!' In each case, rather than analysing the situation and approaching decision-making in the objective way I've suggested here, these people are trusting to lucky breaks rather than exploring the reasons for their floundering companies and failed relationships.

This may sound so obvious that it hardly needs to be said at all. But reflect, honestly, on some of your past choices, and I think you'll have to agree that on at least one occasion you told yourself reassuringly: 'Things just can't go on being as bad as this. I must be due for a lucky break soon.'

Checking Your Choices

When preparing to reach a decision, check your choices by asking these questions:

Why do I have to make a decision?
What is it I have to do?
What plan do I have for dealing with the situation?
What information do I have?
How reliable is my information?
What more information might I need?

Make certain that your chosen course of action does not involve any of the negative management programs described in Step Five of the Alpha Plan.
While making the decision:

* Relax and go into alpha. Mind-mirror different choices, and explore how they might work out, drawing on past experiences but using plenty of right-brain imagination.
  Ask yourself:
* Am I making full use of the information available?
* Am I considering the consequences two or three steps down the road?
* Should I seek more information before making my decisions?
* Have I taken every possible option into account?

Once you have made your choice while mind-mirroring, put that decision into practice. Having done so, ask yourself:

* What aspects were helpful or unhelpful?
* How might I have improved my decision?
* Do I need more information before making a similar decision?

By following these simple steps, you should find your ability to make all kinds or decisions, especially those of major importance to yourself and family, greatly enhanced.

Alpha Action-Plan Three: Problem-solving

'To understand is hard. Once one understands, action is easy.'

Sun Yat Sen

Problem-solving is a way of adapting to change. Animals survive by solving problems, and humans have come to dominate the earth because we are the world's supreme problem-solving species. Not only do we seek answers to present problems but we can look forward in time, work out what may happen and then visualise appropriate solutions well in advance. You can do this even more efficiently when relaxed and in the alpha state.

Check Your Evidence

Start by testing the information on which you will be basing your solution, since any errors at this point must, inevitably, result in wrong answers. If your solution is to be based on numerical data be absolutely certain that you understand their meaning before you begin. Make life easier for yourself, unless you are an experienced mathematician or statistician, by following these simple procedures:

* Simplify and round all numbers. Unless given good reasons, which you fully understand, for not

eliminating any decimal points do so. For example, 3.67 and 5.21 can be understood and used more easily if changed into 4 and 5, without significant loss of accuracy.

* Ignore all evidence consisting of a single number. To have any value, figures must nearly always be compared.
* Check the logic of conclusions based on statistics with special care.
* Insist on knowing how and by whom the statistics were collected. Check that they have been checked.
* If you don't understand the numbers say so and refuse to proceed further until you do.

Define The Problem

Start by stating your problem clearly and concisely. It will help to clarify your thinking if you write it down. Ask: 'What do I know and where do I want to go?'

Many people fail to solve problems because they do not understand their true goal. A female executive once complained that she found it difficult to assert herself with male subordinates. She assumed that her problem was lack of assertiveness, but in reality it was an inability to assert herself without being regarded as unfeminine. Since there were occasions when this proved impossible, she had to rethink her goals before it was possible to come up with an effective answer.

Use Alpha When Seeking Answers

Go into alpha and imagine confronting that problem and coming up with as many different solutions as possible, no matter how wild and improbable they may at first seem. Employ the same procedure described for exploring decisions. Free-wheel possible answers for a while, before editing your ideas and rejecting any which are truly impossible. Examine the remainder carefully. Among them could be the solution you seek. Ask yourself whether an operation which is of no practical value as currently stated might not be utilised if considered in a different light.

Focus on one idea and mind-mirror the different ways it might be changed or modified. Visualise the colour, shape, size, smell or movement being altered in some way. Imagine it reversed, turned upside down or put back to front. Perform a mind experiment in which you are combining two or more of your ideas, and then making them bigger, or more complicated, giving them greater speed or strength. See what might happen if you were to change the weight, thickness, or frequency, if it was smaller, simpler, weaker or more compact. Picture it made from other materials, or using different processes. Can an idea be adapted, built up or broken down? Take one idea and imagine it in an entirely different context.

Avoid tunnel vision, when reviewing possible solutions, by considering any further problems which may arise as you put your solution into effect. If any difficulties are likely to occur, how can they best be avoided or resolved?

Ask yourself:

Am I absolutely clear about the goal I seek?
Are there other equally valid goals?
Are my emotions influencing my judgement of the situation?

Controlling Your Emotions

The next time you have a tricky problem to solve, keep notes of the actions you reviewed and the feelings you have while searching for the solution. From your notes identify positive and negative programs. Positive programs might include, 'I think I can understand this problem', 'I seldom have much difficulty with this sort of problem'; negative programs could be, 'I'm hopeless at this sort of task', 'My brain can't cope with these problems'.

Now count up the number of action and management programs you recorded. Effective problem-solving means generating *three* times as many action programs as positive management programs while avoiding all negative programs. Positive management programs, in moderation, help boost confidence and enhance motivation. But occupy your mind with too many of them and concentration on the practical aspects of problem-solving is harmed.

Problem-solving and Creative Thinking

Many problems can be solved more readily, or prevented from arising, if you are willing to set aside 15 to 20 minutes each day during which you do nothing else but think.

Relax, go into alpha and – if this helps – listen to some music. Allow your brain to range freely without inhibiting your thoughts. Record ideas as they come into your mind, and at the end of each session discard those which are obviously unrealistic. Transfer ideas to index cards, one idea per card, and file them under appropriate headings. Review these cards from time to time. You may well find that, by bringing together a number of solutions, you come up with extremely effective answers to complex problems.

Alpha Action-Plan Four: Managing Stress

'No good work is ever done while the heart is hot and anxious and fretted.'

Olive Schreiner

The Challenge of Stress

Stress can be friend or foe. When allowed to take control of your life it creates management and action programs very likely to undermine performance, destroy happiness and ruin health. Yet the same circumstances which generate these negative responses can also be used to create programs which enhance mental and physical performance. By reprograming your mind to manage stress effectively, you should find it possible to become healthier, happier and more successful.

The essential point to bear in mind is that each of us has a Peak Performance Stress Level (PPSL), which varies in magnitude from one task to the next. Dr Hans Selye, a pioneer researcher into the effects of stress, has termed the stress associated with peak performance 'eustress' (from the Greek *eu*, meaning 'good', as in the word euphoria) to distinguish it from distress (from the Latin *dis*, meaning 'away from', as in the word disagreement). Your PPSL represents the level of eustress required in order to think or act with maximum efficiency in a particular set of circumstances.

Distress occurs either when the brain is required to process too much information in too little time or when the inputs are reduced to a point where there are too little incoming data to provide adequate stimulation.

Understress, which is usually associated with tedious or routine chores, damages performance and health as badly as the overstress, resulting from excessive intellectual, emotional, or physical demands. Under extreme conditions, when the level of incoming information is drastically restricted, as happens during sensory deprivation experiments or some forms of interrogation, the brain starts to self-stimulate through hallucinations.

While the PPSL is being maintained, eustress ensures that you feel energetic and enthusiastic, cope well with life's demands, have a healthy appetite and enjoy restful sleep. You look forward to the challenge of each new day and feel in control of events.

As stress levels increase you become increasingly anxious, confused, frustrated and uncertain of your ability to cope with the demands being made on your time and energy. You make poor decisions and lack skill or creativity in the solutions sought to important problems. Your memory and concentration falter so that even well learned facts and figures become elusive and such recall as you do achieve is often inaccurate.

When stress levels decrease below optimum, you grow bored, apathetic and lack motivation. You may feel hopeless and depressed, have a poor appetite and sleep badly, although you may feel tired much of the time. Decision-making and problem-solving become harder so that even a simple choice or trivial difficulty can appear to be an insurmountable obstacle. As a result one gets trapped in the downward cycle created by negative programs.

If you are obliged to work above or below the PPSL for any great length of time performance may suffer the

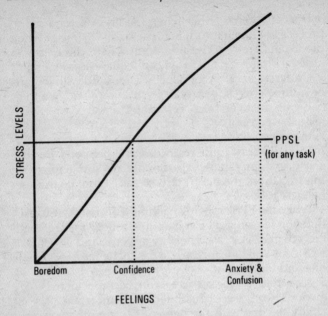

abrupt decline which American researchers have dubbed Burn-Out Stress Syndrome (BOSS).

A pioneer worker in this field, associate professor of psychology at the University of California, Christina Maslach, defines burnout as the 'loss of concern for the people with whom one is working' in response to job-related stress. Another researcher, Cary Chernis, describes it as 'psychological withdrawal from work in response to excessive stress or dissatisfaction. A calling becomes merely a job.' It is the result of high levels of job stress, personal frustration, and inadequate coping skills which involve major personal, organisational and social costs which are probably increasing. Common symptoms include:

* Exhaustion – loss of energy, depletion, debilitation,

fatigue. There is a sharp reduction in trust, interest, feelings and concern for others.

* A decline in personal relationships and negative responses to other people. The sufferer feels increasingly irritable, incapable of coping with minor frustrations and tends to focus on disappointments and failures instead of successes.
* Depression, low morale and feelings of hopelessness.
* Health problems, including upset digestion; aching muscles, especially in the lower back and neck; headaches; and missed menstrual periods.
* An increase in most types of consumption: the victim smokes more cigarettes, drinks more alcohol, takes more drugs (both medically prescribed and otherwise) and, usually, eats more food. The latter symptom can be reversed, however, with the appetite sometimes showing a marked decline.

Once established, BOSS tends to become a self-forcing process, as the negative management and action programs involved tend to produce further discouragement and withdrawal which results in further failure and even greater discouragement and withdrawal.

Assessing Your Stress Levels

You can discover whether or not you are achieving a stress level likely to result in peak performance on any particular activity by thinking about some task which you perform regularly and rating yourself on the PPSL checklist below. If a statement is *very true* you should rate it at 10, if *not true at all* rate it at 0. If the truth lies somewhere between those extremes then give an intermediate rating.

On most occasions when carrying out that task, I
1. Feel enthusiastic.
2. Tackle it energetically.
3. Look forward to undertaking it.
4. Find satisfaction in doing it.
5. Would sooner be doing it than something else.
6. Enjoy myself.
7. Feel relaxed, or pleasurably stimulated.
8. Feel that the investment of time and effort has been worthwhile once the job is done.
9. Consider I achieved most of what I had hoped to achieve.
10. Would feel good about tackling the same task again.

Score	Stress Level
100–80:	You are almost certainly at your PPSL for this task.
79–50:	Your PPSL fluctuates. As a result you probably notice that some parts of the task are accomplished more easily and more successfully than others.
49–20:	A score in this range may mean that your stress level is either somewhat too low or slightly too high. In the first case the task is probably insufficiently challenging. In the second, attempting to cope with excessive demands seem likely to have depleted your mental and physical energy. A change of routine is indicated in either case.
19 – 0:	The remarks made above apply even more strongly when your score comes into this extremely low range. The stress level generated by that activity is totally incompatible with successful performance, unless the task is so simple and routine that it makes few, if any mental or physical demands.

Scoring the PPSL Check List

A rule-of-thumb method for deciding whether you are above or below your PPSL for any particular task is to note whether, when carrying it out, you feel more anxious than apathetic.

As I explained in Chapter Seven, a moderate anxiety level is not only acceptable but actually highly desirable because it helps to tune up both mind and body, making you feel alert without undermining performance. But when anxiety starts making you physically tense and mentally confused, the stress level has risen too high. Equally, the less you care whether the task is done well or badly the lower the stress created.

You can also keep an eye on your stress levels through the use of an easily constructed monitoring device which consists of nothing more complicated than two sheets of plain paper and a piece of carbon paper. This assessment is based on the fact that shifts away from PPSL bring about either a reduction or an increase in the pressure used when writing. The stress monitor allows you to compare these pressures across time.

Constructing the Stress Monitor

This should be done at a time when you feel confident and relaxed. Take two pieces of plain paper and place a sheet of carbon paper between them. Using a Biro write half a dozen words across the centre of the paper. Apply the sort of pressure you would use if writing a letter. This gives you a sample of normal handwriting and can be identified by writing PPSL against it.

Next repeat the sentence at the top of the sheet, this time applying the *lightest* pressure necessary for producing a carbon copy.

Write the sentence a third time at the bottom of the sheet, applying the *heaviest* pressure you can without tearing the paper.

Repeat the sentence a fourth time midway between the top and middle lines – applying a pressure halfway between your lightest and your normal stroke. Identify this with the word 'retreat'. Finally write the sentence between the middle and bottom lines, using a pressure mid-way between normal and heaviest. Identify this with the word 'attack'.

Discard away the top copy, since the greater contrast of the carbon makes it easier to use when monitoring changes in stress levels.

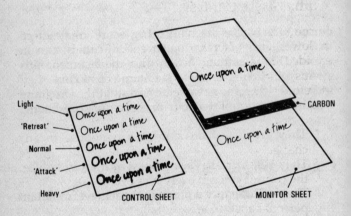

To monitor your stress levels use two sheets of paper, and the carbon as before. Write out the same sentence, using normal pressure, and compare the new and old copies.

If the pressure used on the test sentence corresponds with the PPSL line on the monitor your level of stress has probably not changed all that much across time.

Should the pressure have become lighter, looking more like the line labelled 'retreat', or heavier so that it corresponds more closely to the line marked 'attack', it is likely that you have experienced a shift away from your PPSL.

A lighter stroke suggests a falling level of stress while the heavier pressure indicates rising stress. The former is more likely to bring about a retreat from life, as you become less energetic and involved, while the latter suggests an increasingly aggressive, attacking, approach. In either case steps should be taken to return to the PPSL as quickly as possible.

Alpha Stress Control

Burnout, as well as the many other less dramatic effects of lower-level, short-term, stress difficulties, can be avoided by acquiring action and management programs which enable you to maintain your PPSL.

Before doing so, however, check that the programs you intend to employ satisfy the following conditions:

* They are based on a positive response to any change.
* They will increase, or at worst in no way reduce, the control you can exert over events.
* They will enhance your ability to achieve important personal goals in life.

Ideally such changes should be linked to improvements in the working conditions, such as better on-the-job training; greater recognition of personal effort; carefully graduated levels of responsibility for new staff and steps to ensure that the same staff are not always working overtime. Unfortunately it seldom proves possible for those on the receiving end of bad employment practices to do much to change things for the better.

If you are in a position to reduce workplace stress, then the long-term benefits in terms of both individual employee performance and corporate efficiency are likely to more than justify the extra time, trouble and expenditure involved.

Although the sources of stress in the modern world are many and varied, research suggests that significant shifts away from PPSL are most likely to be caused by three main factors: time pressures, life events and loss of control. Let's take each in turn to see how the changes in stress they generate can be managed more effectively.

Time Pressure Stress

As I have explained, stress rises when too many demands are being made on the brain's processing abilities, just as it falls when there are too few demands.

The crucial factor here is *time*. Imagine that you are trapped in your bedroom by a hotel fire and have to work out a way of escaping. In the first case, with flames blazing in the corridor, you assume that you have only seconds to develop the plan on which your life depends.

Under these conditions a probable reaction is panic. Investigations of emergencies and disasters have shown that less than 25 per cent of those involved responded intelligently. The majority behaved in ways which not only put them in greater danger, but made it harder for others to save them. Some froze, unable to move in any direction. Not long ago a flying instructor friend of mine almost died after his student did just that while piloting a light aircraft. So great was this man's terror that only with extreme difficulty could his hands

be wrenched from the controls and the aircraft pulled
out of its potentially fatal dive. Others go to the
opposite extreme, and indulge in actions which are as
frenetic as they are futile. Firemen report how, in their
terror, some fire survivors plunge to their death rather
than wait a few moments longer for the rescue ladder to
reach them.

Now imagine the same situation. You are again trapped in a hotel room by fire, but this time you know that
the fire door will hold back even the fiercest blaze for as
long as three hours. With more time for your brain to
process all the available information it is much more
likely that you will be able to review a wide range of
options and come up with a life-saving strategy rather
than responding with mindless terror.

Even under less dramatic circumstances, action programs aimed at ensuring effective time management
are an essential part of effective stress management.

The starting point for developing these programs is
clearly to establish a set of major life goals; to create a
plan for your life which provides direction and purpose
by guiding you from short- to medium- to long-term
objectives. The exercises in Step Five were intended to
help you define these major goals more clearly. If you
completed them you should have a good idea of what
you want to achieve in the key areas of life – family,
social, career and leisure. Whenever possible, drop any
activity that takes up your time without helping you
achieve a major goal. If that's too difficult then reduce
your involvement as much as possible to leave more
time free for activities of real importance to you.

Now consider the steps required in order to achieve
those goals. If your plan includes developing a warm
and loving relationship with your partner and being
successful in your career, essential ingredients will
obviously need to include both spending time with
your partner and enhancing your work skills. Organise

your activities according to their importance in helping you achieve those goals. Getting your priorities right makes it easier to decide how best to respond to different demands on your time.

When faced with any task there are only four ways of responding. You can drop it, delay it, delegate it or do it. Action programs which help you make the correct choice are powerful allies when it comes to maintaining PPSL.

Drop It

While this may sound the easiest option of all, changing time-wasting but deeply ingrained habits often demands real dedication; especially if these activities are rewarding and pleasurable, like the extra half-hour in bed, turning on the TV first thing each evening and only turning it off when we go to bed, reading junk mail, lingering over lunch and so on.

If any of these activities has a genuine place in your life plan there's no need to drop it. Instead give that habit a priority rating and then set aside the necessary time when planning your daily timetable. But avoid the trap of getting stuck in a time-wasting rut.

Less easily dropped are time-wasting habits which involve other people: for instance, being sociable with people you don't like all that much. Ask yourself whether such activities as chatting to boring Beryl or listening to the endless problems of moaning Mike will help you achieve a goal in life. If it does then, as before, assign that activity a priority in your schedule. If not, then drop it as quickly as possible. Any guilt you experience is a small price to pay for the time saved.

Delay It

There are two sorts of delay. Negative delay, commonly called procrastination and positive delay, which actually makes you function more efficiently by saving time, energy and effort.

It's easy to identify negative delay since it involves replacing a high-priority activity with one of much lower priority. Psychologists sometimes refer to this as a displacement activity. For instance, you know that you ought to prepare a difficult report, but instead you waste time on the low-priority task of tidying your desk.

Positive delay is involved when

* You postpone a low-priority task for one with a high priority.
* You postpone a task which arouses strong emotions, such as anger, depression, bitterness or envy. For instance, your bank manager has just refused to honour a cheque and you decide to write him an angry letter of complaint. Delay here, until your anger has diminished, could prove both a time- and a face-saver.
* You have insufficient information or lack the requisite amount of skill to undertake the task efficiently. Delay here, while you gain the necessary knowledge, will save waste of time and needless errors.
* Your physical or mental state are such that it seems unlikely that you could carry out the job successfully; for instance, feeling too jet-lagged, after flying the Atlantic, to make sound decisions.

Delegate It

Effective delegation is one of the greatest time-savers there is. Not only does it allow you to assign more time to tasks which only you can perform, it probably means that you'll get a better job done all round. Equally, it is important not to take on other people's work, or allow them to burden you with their responsibilities. Practise saying 'no' to unreasonable requests. Use mind-mirroring to help you here if your natural inclination is to agree to almost anything rather than assert yourself.

Do It

It is at this stage that many people come unstuck. Although they have clearly identified a high-priority job they can never find the right moment to begin.

As a final chore each evening plan your goals, so far as possible, for the following day. Set aside time for routine tasks and those you simply can't avoid. If possible begin with the more demanding tasks and leave the easier ones until later in the day; that way you'll be investing your energy more efficiently.

Remember Murphy's Law, which states that if something can go wrong it will go wrong and that everything takes longer than you think. Give yourself room for manoeuvre by setting aside more time than you hope will be needed. But keep some lower priority, less time-demanding, tasks in reserve should you complete the really important tasks quicker than anticipated. Minor chores which you can fit in between major activities help you make the most of every moment.

While it's important to do every job to the best of your ability, you must also recognise when the time has come to down tools and move to the next assignment. Attempting to achieve needless perfection when the results already achieved are perfectly satisfactory is actually a negative delaying tactic. Your work plan must be sufficiently flexible to cope with the unexpected. The unscheduled meeting, the unexpected visit from an important client, the surprise party invitation, that last-minute panic at work and so on. This is where setting yourself clearly defined goals proves so helpful, since if you are obliged to handle the unexpected or to cope in an emergency, it becomes far easier to decide which of your other tasks can be dropped, delayed or delegated.

Life-event Stress

Major life events, such as moving home, the ending of an important relationship, the serious illness of a loved-one, children leaving home, redundancy or retirement and, especially, bereavement, all create significant increases in stress. Career changes are, not surprisingly, especially stressful to extremely ambitious men and women since their work is often central to their self-identity and self-esteem.

Where such changes are predictable but unpreventable – for example, retirement – it is essential to make plans well in advance so that the transition from one role to another is more progressive than traumatic.

The starting point is to identify the major rewards obtained from a particular role. If it involves having a top-level job within a company, for instance, the rewards are likely to include a good income, status, stimulating intellectual challenges, the opportunity of meeting people, and a sense of pride and satisfaction derived from membership of a powerful and prestigious organisation.

Well before the time comes for all this to change – for instance, through retirement or predictable redundancy – prepare to replace as many as possible of these rewards by seeking out alternative roles. You might decide, for instance, to become involved in local politics, or place your commercial experience at the services of a club or charity; you might embark on an entirely different second career or accept an offer from your old firm to stay on as a part-time consultant; you could opt for a stimulating leisure activity. All are likely to demand new action programs in order to meet the unfamiliar social and intellectual challenges involved.

The sooner one starts acquiring any skills needed the easier and less stressful the transition from one role to another is likely to prove. The key to controlling the stress generated by this type of life event can be summed up in just one word – planning. Start as early as possible because time has a habit of slipping past with remarkable speed, and today is the tomorrow you failed to prepare for yesterday.

Dealing with unexpected changes – the end of a relationship you believed was secure, the loss of a close relative or friend – is generally far more difficult because the stresses created by bereavement and mourning are amongst the most powerful we ever experience.

But, here again, the key to maintaining PPSL is to view the event not as evidence of your personal lack of worth or as divine retribution for an imagined failure on your part, but as one of those bad things which happen to good people.

Never feel embarrassed about being emotional; the stiff upper lip is a barrier to psychological health, not a sign of it. Tears and anger serve as safety valves. Even these seemingly negative emotions can have very positive, life-preserving values. Bear in mind too that it is perfectly natural – and essential – to pass through recognised stages of grieving. These typically start with denial – the initial response of many when told of a loss is to gasp 'Oh, no . . .'; often closely followed by guilt – 'If I had behaved differently this would never have happened' – and anger – 'How could she/he/they do this to me . . .?' As I have said, such responses are entirely to be expected and many psychologists consider that one has to work through each stage in order to come to terms with the loss.

Once the first shock has passed, however, it is essential to stop brooding about what might have been, distance yourself and start searching for any positive features in the change. Review these in terms of your life-plan and seek to replace what has been lost with activities which can produce an equal, if different, level of stimulation.

Loss of Control Stress

The greater the control you are able to exercise over events the easier it is to maintain your PPSL; firstly, because knowing that what you say and do will have a direct influence over what happens both reduces anxiety and increases motivation; secondly because control makes it easier to bring about changes in the working, or home, environment that will reduce, or eliminate needless sources of stress.

There are bound to be some occasions when control is snatched from your grasp so swiftly that you can do little, for the moment, to influence events. Accept that when this happens, through accident or misfortune, you will suffer the adverse effects of uncontrolled stress. The essential thing is to recapture as much control as possible as swiftly as you can. When the going gets rough it is only natural to seek help, advice and support from family and friends. Once the immediate crisis is over, however, it is important to take prompt action to reduce dependency and reassert responsibility for your own life.

More frequently, however, control over events slips from one's grasp more slowly, as the result of many minor incidents rather than one major catastrophe. This usually occurs when a vicious circle develops between loss of control and unhelpful changes in stress levels.

The cycle of decline usually follows this pattern. Something happens that makes it harder for you to control events, and this changes your PPSL for that activity. Because stress is now undermining your performance, the loss of control becomes more substantial.

The shift away from eustress increases, resulting in even greater loss of control. And so the downward cycle continues, and becomes increasingly difficult to break out of.

The answer is to keep a watchful eye on your ability to control events and resist any proposals – however well intentioned – that lessen your freedom of action.

Stress Control and the Alpha Plan

The ability to relax mind and body through a combination of physical exercises and alpha production will help to protect you against many of the harmful effects of excessive stress.

Unwinding, in this way, last thing each day or following some especially stressful encounter, reduces blood pressure, improves digestion, prevents aches and pains from needlessly tense muscles and sustains energy levels by ensuring more restful sleep.

The soothing imagery you have learned to produce during the alpha state will prevent the mind from dwelling unhelpfully on worries, and curtail the negative, circulating, thoughts that clutter the minds of most stressed people, often to the extent of preventing them from thinking clearly and rationally about ways of overcoming those concerns.

The action programs suggested above will help to reduce excessive stress or prevent it from dropping below your PPSL. But to give those programs the best chance of proving effective you will need to manage them – and any other coping strategies which you use – in a positive manner.

Use mind-mirroring to enhance your ability to perform more confidently and effectively in situations which currently cause you stress. Work out how you might respond so as either to reduce or increase the stress created by those challenges.

Consider the alternatives open to you and check each

option against the qualifications, described in Step Five, which are necessary in order to develop a positive management program.

Go into alpha and, as vividly as possible, imagine yourself carrying out this activity. If you find yourself becoming tense or distressed in any way during such a training exercise then, as suggested earlier, switch off that scene and return to the pleasant, relaxing one. When you are calm and again in the alpha state return to that scene and continue working through it as vividly as possible.

For instance, you might realise that a source of stress is your inability to stand up to unreasonable demands. Instead of meekly agreeing to the suggestion that you take on yet more work, what you would really like to do is refuse. The alternative scenarios which might be investigated in this situation could include: outright, terse refusal; making an excuse; putting off having to make a decision; or explaining in a calm but assertive manner exactly why it is impossible for you to agree to that proposal.

Of these, only the last response meets the requirements of a positive management program. It is truthful, defends your own position without attacking anybody else's, it is honest and it is relevant to your needs. Picture yourself behaving in this new way, imagine how other people might respond and how you would feel before, during and after the event.

Once you have rehearsed the scene in alpha a few times the next step is to put it into practice in real life. Use the rapid relaxation exercise to help you keep physically calm, especially when contemplating the activity. Afterwards, use the performance analysis procedure described in Step Three of the Plan to identify the strengths and weaknesses of that approach. Remember to focus on the positive as well as any negative aspects of your behaviour.

Alpha Action-Plan Five:
Physical Fitness

'Take care of the means, and the end will take care of itself.'

Mahatma Gandhi

It may seem curious to include a section on physical fitness in a book whose intention is to help you achieve peak mental performance. Yet the truth is that our brain can only function at maximum efficiency so long as the body is maintained in a healthy condition. By that I don't mean that you have to be fit enough to run a marathon; merely that your system should, as nearly as possible, be functioning as nature intended.

As the positive and negative fitness cycles show, mental, emotional and bodily well-being are all closely related to one another.

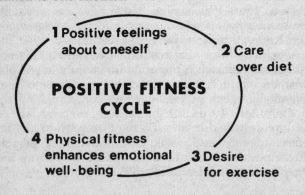

1 Positive feelings about oneself

2 Care over diet

POSITIVE FITNESS CYCLE

4 Physical fitness enhances emotional well-being

3 Desire for exercise

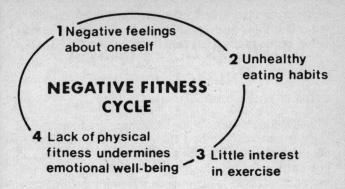

The trouble is, of course, that much of what we do in our daily life conflicts nature's intentions. The human body was designed for action and movement; muscles need to be stretched and worked to remain in good shape, just as the brain must be given regular intellectual work-outs to operate effectively. Unfortunately many people spend more time sitting than exercising and riding than walking.

As I have already explained, the Alpha Plan assists in improving and maintaining physical health by greatly reducing stress levels. But you can enhance these procedures still further by setting aside no more than fifteen minutes per day, a few times each week, for improving your physical condition. By doing so you will not only increase stamina, build muscle tone, and strengthen your cardiovascular system, thereby enhancing all aspects of bodily function; you will also further improve both intellectual performance and emotional health.

One effect of exercise, for instance, is to raise the level of endorphins circulating in the blood. These are the natural opiates responsible for producing the 'jogger's high' – those powerful and pleasurable sensations that help make running so addictive. Endorphins may also assist in alleviating depression and anxiety. Certainly it is far healthier to exercise away tensions, rather than either bottle them up or vent them in periodic bursts of anger and frustration.

Fitness in Fifteen Minutes a Day

Physical fitness starts at the fingertips. Use them to find out how fit you are and then use this knowledge to create a program exactly suited to your age, sex and current level of training. By adopting this approach you not only feel fitter faster but actually enjoy training your body to perform more efficiently.

The heart is an extremely sensitive health computer, with its read out – pulse rate – giving an accurate

---

How To Take Your Pulse

Rest your left wrist in the right palm so that it lies between the thumb and forefinger. The tips of the third and fourth finger of your right hand are now positioned above the pulse.

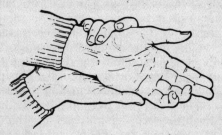

Press lightly and you should detect it easily. If you have difficulty move your fingers slightly until the pulse is felt. For accuracy, count the beats over 15 seconds and multiply the result by 4 to give beats per minute.

indication of cardiac performance, the key to fitness. To read the heart's health message proceed as follows.

Sit down and relax for 10–15 minutes before taking your pulse (see box for details). For most people the resting pulse rate is about 70 beats per minute, but for somebody in peak condition, such as a trained athlete, the rate can be as low as 40. The slower the resting heart the fitter you are. Write down this rate.

You are now ready to take the fitness factor test. This lasts only six minutes, but the movements should be rehearsed to ensure that you can perform them smoothly.

Because this test makes your heart work harder than normal you should seek medical advice before attempting it, if you are in a poor physical condition and unused to taking much exercise; seriously over-weight; suffer from a heart trouble or high blood pressure; experience dizzy spells; are aged sixty plus; or recently underwent surgery. If in any doubt please consult your GP before continuing.

The Test

Remove tight clothing and either take off your shoes or wear flat ones.

Stand at the bottom of a flight of stairs, feet together, one hand resting on the banister for support. The movements you will be executing during the fitness factor test are as follows: As shown in the illustration, place your right foot on the first stair. Lift your left foot to the second stair. Put your right foot beside the left.

Now go down the steps again, reversing the movements as you do so. Left foot on first stair, right foot to the floor. Finally the left foot is placed beside the right on the floor.

This sequence must be repeated for *three minutes* with the rhythm: *up-two-three, down-two-three, up-two-three*.

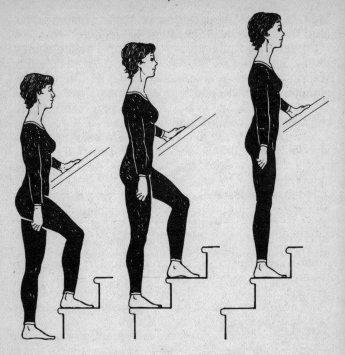

The movement of each foot constitutes one step and the number of steps you must take during the three-minute test period varies according to your age and sex. See Fig. 7, above.

You will find it easier to keep count of the steps and maintain the correct rhythm if the 3 minutes are divided into 12 periods of 15 seconds. Where possible, work with a friend and have him, or her, signal each time period so that you don't have to glance at your watch all the time. It's important to keep moving throughout the 3-minute period.

Continue for the full three minutes unless you start to

Fig. 7 Number Of Steps To Take In Three Minutes		
Your Age	*Steps Every 15 Secs*	*Total In 3 Min*
Women:		
15–39	26	312
40–49	21	252
50 +	16	192
Men:		
15–29	33	396
30–39	29	348
40–49	26	312
50 +	18	216

feel breathless, dizzy or over-tired, in which case *stop* immediately. This indicates that your current fitness level appears inadequate for what is, of necessity, a demanding test. I suggest that you start taking more exercise on a regular basis – walking instead of riding, for instance – for a couple of weeks and then attempt the test again. It might also prove advisable to undergo a medical check-up.

At the end of three minutes take your pulse again. If it is *faster* than those listed in Fig. 8 below, *stop* the test at this point and award yourself five points. Work out the recovery rate, and calculate your exercise goal using the procedure described overleaf.

Fig. 8 Maximum pulse for continuing with test		
These apply to both sexes		
Age	*Rate After 3 Min*	*Action*
15–30	170 +	STOP
31–40	160 +	STOP
41–50	150 +	STOP
51–60	140 +	STOP
61 +	130 +	STOP

Start the second part of the test only if your pulse rate is lower than the figures listed for your age group in the table above.

This time, to make your heart work harder, you must add 12 steps during each 15-second period, a total of 144 additional steps over the 3 minutes. As before, stop at once should you become breathless or feel dizzy. If this happens award yourself 8 points and calculate the recovery rate and exercise goal as explained below.

After the second 3-minute test period is completed take your pulse and obtain your exercise score from Fig. 9 below.

Fig. 9 Exercise Score		
Age	*Pulse After 2nd Test period*	*Score*
15–29	156 or more	10
	155 or less	20
30–40	150 or more	10
	149 or less	20
41–50	144 or more	10
	143 or less	20
51 +	138 or more	10
	137 or less	20

Now Calculate Your Recovery Rate

The recovery rate is the time needed by your heart to return to normal after the test. Work this out as follows. One minute after finishing the test take your pulse again. Subtract this from the rate immediately after the end of the test and ignore the last number. For example:

Pulse rate at end of fitness factor test = 140
Pulse rate 60 seconds after the test = 90
Difference (140–90) = 50 Recovery rate = 5

To discover your fitness factor you must perform one final calculation. Multiply your test score by your recovery rate to arrive at an overall fitness score. For example:

Exercise Score = 20; Recovery Rate = 5;
  Fitness score = 100
Exercise Score = 10; Recovery Rate = 3;
  Fitness score = 30

Use Fig. 10, below, to obtain the fitness factor indicated by this final score and to find out what it says about your current level of physical well-being.

Fig. 10 Fitness Factor		
Final Score	Fitness Factor	Condition
5–39	.5	Poor
40–79	.6	Fair
80–100	.7	Very Good
100 +	.8	Excellent

Because a number of calculations were needed to arrive at the fitness factor let me just run through the procedure once more:

1. Relax for a few moments and take your resting pulse. Note this down.
2. Perform the step test. Use Fig. 7 to find out how many steps you should do during the first session, based on your age and sex. Stop after the first session if your pulse rate exceeds those given in Fig. 8. For the second 3-minute session add an extra 144 steps over the 3-minute period. Obtain your exercise score from Fig. 9.

3. Take your pulse at the end of the test and 60 seconds later. Subtract the second rate from the first and forget the final number to give you the recovery rate.

4.   Calculate your fitness score by multiplying the exercise score (from Fig. 9) by your recovery rate. Use this final score to obtain your fitness factor, and an indication of your current physical condition, from Fig. 10.

With your fitness factor identified you now create a training schedule which takes this fully into account. By doing so you'll progress to a high level of physical health with none of the uncomfortable puffing and panting caused by a haphazard approach to training.

You may train with *any* type of exercise so long as it raises your pulse heart rate to a level determined by your age and your fitness factor. This is called the exercise goal. To work out this goal one final, calculation is required.

Calculating Your Exercise Goal

To do this you take your age away from 220 and multiply the result by the fitness factor (a calculator may help here). This produces the pulse rate exercise goal.

For example, Peter is forty-five years old and obtained a fitness factor of 0.6, which shows him to be in fair physical condition. His exercise goal, therefore, becomes:

$$(220 - 45) \times 0.6 = 105 \text{ beats per minute}$$

Mary, aged thirty, achieved a 0.7 fitness factor, indicating that she is in much better shape. Her exercise goal calculates at:

$$(220 - 30) \times 0.7 = 133 \text{ beats per minute}$$

Creating Your Fitness Program

The choice of activity employed to raise your pulse rate to the required level is up to you. The only consideration is that it sustains the increase needed for a full fifteen minutes. This means that jogging, running, fast walking, skipping, disco dancing, cycling, roller skating, ice skating, rowing (machine or actual boat) and the static bike are all excellent. Tennis and squash could be included provided you are able to monitor your pulse rate and maintain it at very close to the required exercise goal.

Making the heart work too hard – producing too rapid a pulse rate – is as unhelpful as making it work too little.

Choose the activity you find most pleasurable, possibly ringing the changes from time to time to prevent boredom. Make sure that each session lasts the full fifteen minutes and try to have at least three, and preferably four or five, such sessions every week. That's all it takes to return you to a first-class state of fitness, building stamina, improving the circulation, enhancing muscle health, strengthening your heart and shedding excess fat.

At the first start take your pulse every few minutes to ensure that the right level has been achieved and is being maintained. If it is too low, work that much harder; if it rises too high then slow down immediately. After a while you'll find it easy to spot when you are putting exactly the right amount of effort into your exercising to reach and maintain the required rate.

After a few weeks, take the fitness factor test again. You'll almost certainly find that it has improved considerably. This means that you will need to recalculate your exercise goal and then work that little bit harder to achieve the new, higher, pulse rate.

Peak Performance

So far we have considered sports as a means to an end: that of enhancing fitness. But, as I have already explained, the Alpha Plan can also be the means for improving performance when playing any type of sports.

Mind-mirroring enables you to rehearse bodily movements mentally before attempting them in real life. By doing so you should increase the speed and accuracy of muscle control, improve your powers of observation and reduce the inhibiting effects of anxiety, especially when playing under stressful conditions.

During the 1980 Olympics in Moscow, for example, swimmer Duncan Goodhew performed just such a fantasy rehearsal before being called to the starting block. Eyes closed, he vividly imagined the race, split second by split second, stroke by stroke, feeling as well as seeing his progress through the water.

But by linking the power of mirroring with physical relaxation and the alpha state, followed by real-life practice, it is often possible to achieve what racing drivers call a flow state: that perfect union between mind and body, or man and machine, in which split-second decisions become automatic. 'It's when you know what you have to go after, and that's all that matters,' says Mario Andretti. 'Anything else is a distraction.' Benny Parsons comments: 'Everything is under control. The world is at your fingertips, and you're revolving it any way you want to.' Similar ideas are frequently expressed by leading performers in a wide range of sports. In *The Inner Game of Tennis*, W. Timothy Gallwey suggests:

> If you reflect upon your own highest moments or peak experiences . . . you will probably remember them as moments of great pleasure, even ecstasy.

During such experiences the mind does not act like a separate entity telling you what you should do or criticising how you do it. It is quiet: you are 'together', and the action flows free as a river.

A feature of flow states is their time distortion, which means that even rapid, complex actions feel as if they are being performed in slow motion. 'The monitoring of time is primarily a left-hemisphere activity,' says Dr Brad Hatfield of Arizona State University, who believes that the jogger's high, referred to above, may represent a flow state. He points out that, during flow states, the right hemisphere becomes more dominant. 'We know from EEG recordings that left-hemisphere activity becomes reduced, so it's not surprising that its time monitoring capabilities are inhibited.'

Dr Richard Suinn, of Colorado State University – the psychologist usually credited with introducing the practice of visualisation into sports training – makes the point that:

> . . . imaging may have to do with a transfer of what you have in left-hand brain learning into right-brain storage. Flow, then, approximates a state in which information is stored so well in the right brain that you don't have to use the left to trigger it to become active.

By using the Alpha Plan to enhance sports skills it may well prove possible to enjoy what psychologist Abraham Maslow termed 'peak experiences', those marvellous moments when everything comes together and we perform with effortless assurance and absolute success, not on rare occasions but merely by an effort of will; we attain, on demand, that perfect union between mind and body which is both the cause and the consequence of peak performance.

'As soon as we reflect, deliberate, and conceptualise, the original unconsciousness is lost and a thought interferes,' writes D. T. Suzuki, describing the influence of the conscious mind on archery in his forword to *Zen in the Art of Archery*. 'Calculation, which is miscalculation sets in . . .'

This achievement, through conscious and directed effort, of the ability to perform any activity, intellectual or physical, with unconscious perfection, effortlessly, confidently and consistently, is the goal and purpose of the Alpha Plan.

Appendix One

The range of activities which can be enhanced through the Alpha Plan is still being investigated. As I explained in Chapter One, my experience is that it can improve virtually any type of performance. But research is still progressing, and I invite you to participate in these studies by completing the Research Form below.

RESEARCH FORM

To avoid spoiling the book, this page should either be copied or photocopied. All information will be treated in strict confidence. Please return the completed form to: Dr David Lewis, 22 Queen Anne Street, London W1.

Your name..(Dr,Mr,Mrs,Ms)
Your Address...
Date of birth .... Occupation ....

Please give brief details of the activity on which you wished to improve performance using the Alpha Plan.

Please rate how helpful you found the procedures taught in the five-step program, by rating each on a scale of 1–5 where 1 = very helpful and 5 = not helpful at all.

Procedure   Rating
* Physical Relaxation
* Alpha Training

* Performance Analysis
* Mind-mirroring
* Real-life practice

How long did you practice each before moving to the next?

Procedure   Time Spent
* Physical Relaxation
* Alpha Training
* Performance Analysis
* Mind-mirroring
* Real-life practice

To what extent has using the Alpha Plan improved your performance on the target activity? (Please tick as appropriate).

☐ Very Much   ☐ Somewhat   ☐ No Improvement

Please identify any additional benefits by ticking as appropriate:

☐ Less anxious   ☐ Less stressed   ☐ More confident
☐ Better memory   ☐ Improved study methods
☐ Better decision-making   ☐ Better problem-solving
☐ Improved physical health

Any others (please give brief details):

Many thanks for your help.

Appendix Two

A relaxation cassette teaching all the procedures described in Step One of the Alpha Plan has been recorded by Dr Lewis and can be obtained from Stresswatch, 22 Queen Anne Street, London W1. The price is £6.95 including tax, postage and packing.

Bibliography

Albrecht, K. (1980) *Brain Power*; Englewood Cliffs, N.J., Prentice-Hall.

Amosov, N. M. (1967) *Modelling of Thinking and the Mind*; London, Macmillan and Co.

Apter, M. J. (1970) *The Computer Simulation of Behaviour*; London, Hutchinson.

Arbib, M. A. (1972) *The Metaphorical Brain*; New York, John Wiley.

Benoit, H. (1955) *The Supreme Doctrine: Psychological Studies in Zen Thought*; New York, Viking Press.

Boden, M. (1977) *Artificial Intelligence and Natural Man*; Brighton, Harvester Press.

Brown, B. B. (1974) *New Mind, New Body*; London, Hodder and Stoughton.

Cade, M. C. and Coxhead, N. (1983) *The Awakened Mind*; Middlesex, Wildwood House.

Capra, F. (1975) *The Tao of Physics*; New York, Wildwood.

Chaitow, L. (1984) *Relaxation and Meditation Techniques*; New York, Thorsons.

Christie, M. J. and Mellett, P. (Eds) (1981) *Foundations of Psychosomatics*; Chichester, John Wiley.

Davis, G. A. (1973) *Psychology of Problem Solving*; New York, Basic Books.

Dickson, D. N. (1983) *Using Logical Techniques for Making Better Decisions*; New York, John Wiley.

Edwards, B. (1979) *Drawing on the Right Side of the Brain*; London, Souvenir Press.

Fodor, J. A. (1984) *The Modularity of Mind*; Cambridge, Massachusetts, MIT Press.

Funderburk, J. (1977) *Science Studies Yoga*; Himalayan International Institute of Yoga Science and Philosophy, USA.

Gallwey, W. T. (1974) *The Inner Game of Tennis*; London, Jonathan Cape.

Gardner, H. (1983) *Frames of Mind: Theories of Multiple Intelligences*; New York, Basic Books.

Gatchel, R. J. and Price, K. P. (1979) *Clinical Applications of Biofeedback: Appraisal and Status*; New York, Pergamon Press.

Gazzaniga, M. and Blakemore, C. (Eds) (1975) *Handbook of Psychobiology*; New York, Academic Press.

George, F. H. (1980) *Problem Solving*; London, Duckworth.

George, F. H. (1981) *Cybernetics*; London, Hodder and Stoughton.

Gray, J. A. (1982) *The Neurophysiology of Anxiety*; New York, Oxford University Press.

Green, E. and Green, A. (1977) *Beyond Biofeedback*; New York, Delacorte Press.

Hall, E. T. (1984) *The Dance of Life: The Other Dimensions of Time*; New York, Anchor Press.

Hayes, J. R. (1981) *The Complete Problem Solver*; Philadelphia, Franklin Institute.

Holroyd, S. (1983) *The Quest of the Quiet Mind: The Philosophy of Krishnamurti*; Wellingborough, Aquarian Press.

Hulse, S. H., Deese, J. and Egeth, H. (1975) *The Psychology of Learning*; Tokyo, McGraw-Hill Kogakusha Ltd.

Johnson-Laird, P. N. and Wason, P. C. (Eds) (1980) *Thinking: Readings in Cognitive Science*; Cambridge, Cambridge University Press.

Judson, H. F. (1980) *The Search for Solutions*; London, Hutchinson.

Karlins, M. and Andrews, L. M. (1975) *Biofeedback*; London, Abacus.

Keyes, K. (1975) *Handbook To Higher Consciousness*; USA, Living Love Centre.

Leigh, A. (1983) *Decisions, Decisions*; London, Institute of Personnel Management.

Lewis, D. and Greene, J. (1982) *Thinking Better*; New York, Rawson Wade.

Lilly, J. C. (1974) *The Human Biocomputer*; London, Abacus.

Luria, A. R. (1966) *Higher Cortical Functions in Man*; New York, Plenum Press.

Luria, A. R. (1966) *Human Brain and Psychological Processes*; New York, Harper and Row.

Luria, A. R. (1973) *The Working Brain*; Harmondsworth, Penguin Books.

Luria, A. R. (1973) *The Neuropsychology of Memory*; Moscow, Pedagogik Publishing House (Russian); New York (1976).

Martin, I. and Venables, P. H. (1980) *Techniques in Psychophysiology*; Chichester, John Wiley.

McGuigan, F. J., Sime, W. E. and Wallace, J. M. (Eds) (1984) *Stress and Tension Control 2*; New York, Plenum Press.

Meares, A. (1984) *The Wealth Within*; Bath, Ashgrove Press.

Meichenbaum, D. (1979) *Cognitive Behaviour Modification*; New York, Plenum Press.

Michie, D. (1982) *Machine Intelligence and Related Topics*; New York, Gordon and Breach.

Oatley, K. (1978) *Perceptions and Representations*; London, Methuen.

Peper, E., Ancoli, S., and Quinn, M. (Eds) (1981) *Mind/Body Integration*; New York, Plenum Press.

Perkins, D. N. (1981) *The Mind's Best Work*; Cambridge, Massachusetts, Harvard University Press.

Polya, G. (1957) *How To Solve It*; New York, Anchor Books.

Popper, K. R. and Eccles, J. C. (1977) *The Self and Its Brain*; New York, Springer International.

Radford, J. and Burton, A. (1974) *Thinking: Its Nature and Development*; Chichester, John Wiley.

Ruggiero, V. R. (1984) *The Art of Thinking*; New York, Harper and Row.

Shapiro, D., Stoyva, J., Kamiya, J., Barber, T. X., Miller, N. E., and Schwartz, G. E. (1980) *Biofeedback and Behavioural Medicine*; New York, Aldine.

Sheikh, A. A. (Ed) (1983) *Imagery: Current Theory, Research, and, Application*; New York, John Wiley.

Suzuki, D. T. (1985) *Essays in Zen Buddhism*; London, Hutchinson.

Tart, C. T. (1969) *Altered States*; New York, Doubleday and Co.

Tyler, L. E. (1983) *Thinking Creatively*; San Francisco, Jossey-Bass.

Venables, P. H. and Christies, M. J. (Eds) (1975) *Research in Psychophysiology*; New York, John Wiley.

Waddington, C. H. (1977) *Tools for Thought*; St Albans, Paladin.

Weizenbaum, J. (1984) *Computer Power and Human Reason*; Harmondsworth, Penguin Books.

Wickelgren, W. A. (1974) *How To Solve Problems*; San Francisco, W. H. Freeman and Co.

Yazdani, M. and Narayanan, A. (1984) *Artificial Intelligence*; Chichester, Ellis Horwood.

Young, J. Z. (1978) *Programmes of the Brain*; Oxford, Oxford University Press.

Index